Comments on Setbacks to Comebacks

Nishit Lal has deeply examined the psyche of achievers and dreamers, and the ideas expressed in the book go beyond the ordinary success recipes. People, particularly those with cerebral inclinations, will find the book enlightening, and it can help the enterprising youngsters to attain the goals which they strive for.

–**Amod Kanth,** Former IPS, DGP

Mr Nishit Lal's new book 'Setbacks to Comebacks' presents an algorithm for success to Young Professionals, who have undergone some perceived setbacks in life. Though success is attributed to be a state of mind, the author has drawn a well laid down path to attain it in a limited number of measured steps. This has been substantiated with interesting anecdotes and apt real life incidents from the lives of successful persons.

According to the Author, the algorithm for success is in the following sequence: identification of goals, setting up quantifiable and measurable goals, fixing a realistic time frame for achieving them followed by the mobilization of resources at one's command and pursuing the goal with the eternal belief determination of achieving it with positivism . The Author has said that the first step of achieving your Goal will be accomplished 50% by reading the Book. This is not an exaggeration.

– **Chander Mohan, IAS,** Chief Secretary, Puducherry

Having seen Nishit grow up from a naughty and full - of - life youngster into someone who conducts workshops on life skills makes me extremely proud and humbled at the same time. The way he goes about achieving his own goals is reflected in this book, and that in itself is a source of inspiration. Nishit has rightly put across the fact that when you visualize you begin to materialize and that everything in life manifests first in the mind and then in reality. His principles are simple yet powerful. Congratulations, Nishit, and I hope this book gets all the appreciation it deserves.

–**Suman Nalwa,** Addl. Dy. Commissioner of Police,
Special Police Unit for Women & Children and Author

Through a series of seemingly complex topics and tool such as NLP, the book lays down simple ground rules for achieving success. Written in a lucid style, it is hard to believe that this is the handiwork of a debutant author.

– **Abhinav Prakash,** HR, Bain & Company, India

A beautiful book... 'Setbacks to Comebacks' gives a step by step process to achieving your goals and living out your dreams. I have always believed in the sheer power of the human spirit, which constantly seeks to rise, above every obstacle, above pain and grief and it is this power that Nishit seeks to awaken. All the best to him for this lovely work.

–**Rashmi Anand,** Author and Counsellor for women undergoing domestic violence

Every page of Setbacks to Comebacks gives you powerful insights on principles of Achievement. Nishit has done a great job of presenting the new ways of maximizing Human potential. A must read.

–**Rajesh Sharma,** Project Manager, Infosys Technologies Limited

Simple and executable insights to realize your true hidden potential and achieve what you can!

–**Sumit Sood,** Account Manager, HCL

This is a collection of tools and strategies to succeed and achieve great results. A very practical book with tools that can be implemented in professional and personal life for success.

–**Manoj Kumar Bhagat,** Asst. Professor OB and HR, Lal Bahadur Shastri Institute of Management.

The Secrets of Peak Performance

Setbacks

To

Comebacks

Nishit Lal

WVPD

Wisdom Village (Publications Division)

Knowledge is information. Wisdom is transformation.

A WVPD PRESENTATION
Books from Wisdom Village (Publications Division) envision to enhance and enrich their readers with life changing experiences from the business, mind, body and soul genres. They strive towards holistic development.

Editorial Coordinator Anu Anand

ISBN 978 93 80710 150

Published in 2011 by:

WVPD

Wisdom Village (Publications Division)
Knowledge is information. Wisdom is transformation.

WVPD is a part of Wisdom Village
649, O4U, Udyog Vihar, Phase V, Gurgaon, Haryana -122001
www.wvpd.in

To Book Your Orders:
Email: wvpdindia@gmail.com
Or Call: +91 9810800469

Published by Anu Anand for WVPD;
Cover Design & Page Setting by Sunil Mathur;
Printed by J.K. Offset Graphics (P) ltd, C-21, O.I.A, Phase-1, New Delhi-20.

ACKNOWLEDGEMENT

This book may not have been possible without the blessings of my father Dr A.K. Lal and my mother Mini Lal. Their support was tremendous and empowering for me. I would also like to thank my masi, Suman Nalwa for gifting me my first self-help book which changed my Life massively. I also present my humble thanks to the publishers of the book, Wisdom Village, Gurgaon and specially Anu Anand for her support and guidance in the process.

I thank all the students who have been part of my seminars. You challenged me to set new benchmarks for myself and made me learn so much. The interaction with you all, was very empowering for me.

Lastly, I also thank someone whom I met in 2005 during my engineering days, you were an angel to me; though our interaction was short you made a big Breakthrough in my Life. Thank you for showing me the way to my Destiny, you will always be remembered.

This book is dedicated to all the empowered souls who have gone beyond their circle of comfort and sought a Life they have so keenly desired.

I salute them!

PREFACE

Breakthroughs in our lives occur when we move from setbacks to the greatest comebacks. We, in our busy schedules, journeys, appointments often tend to forget that we are limitless beings, and Life is meant to be phenomenal. Let me tell you upfront that our greatest fear in life is not Death but the greatest fear is that we did not use the Unlimited Potential that we are born with, which has the power to change our Lives almost instantaneously in any circumstance.

I have personally seen and read about people who on their deathbeds realized that they forgot to live their dreams. Minutes begin turning into days, days into weeks and then months and finally their best years passed by without them getting to know the real secret of achieving results. Many of them shared that they took the wrong turn in their lives only for that short term fruit and compromised a great deal of riches which were destined for them. Getting into an unknown territory was way too difficult, taking risks was a long distance option, setting a definite pathway to their dreams seemed impossible, persistence was a word which was as new as nano technology, security is what they needed in times of change. Each one of them had something in their hearts which they took to their graveyards and then one after the other every dream, each desire, all the "should and could haves" surfaced as the man breathed his last breaths. He took away those unfulfilled dreams and desires, those potential loving relationships that he could have forged, the passion that he kept inside, with him. Everything happened to him because he buried his potential deep into the Earth long before he himself got buried. This book, is about taking out that potential which can revolutionalize your circumstances and create winning moments towards your path of unlimited Success.

The science of getting to Peak Performances is so interesting that as we tend to delve more into it the void of knowledge gets bigger and bigger – the more you read this subject the more you want to know. From the contemporary Success formulas like Neuro Linguistic Programming to the ancient Religious teachings, the formula has been weaved into Seven Principles of getting what you want in Life. It is about You, your Choices, Dreams, Passions, Goals, Emotions, Beliefs, Mental Models, Attraction and last but not the least the most essential ingredient to the curry of Living a fulfilling Life – Your Potential.

Nishit Lal

Table of Contents

Transform Your Life Through Powerful Goals

Are you living by chance or living with an intention? There is a gigantic difference between the two! Living by chance is very unintelligent, a fool can live that way, because he doesn't know where he is going, what is happening around – it is very easy. Leaders live with an intention to make a difference, it is hard and tiring, but it is extremely rewarding. It is not in the achievement of Goal where the reward is found; instead it is in the Journey where the gift lies. Accomplishing your Goal is like accomplishing your life and fulfilling your purpose of being on this planet.

Goal, Goal, Goal
Rock 'N' Roll

"People with goals succeed because they know where they are going. It's as simple as that."
Earl Nightingale

The quality of your life will be determined by the quality of your Goals. Any human achievement in any sphere of life is ascertained by the direction of one's talents and potential towards an aim. No one goes to the airport and asks the lady sitting at the ticket counter, "Mam, could you please give me a ticket?", because she does not know where you wish to GO! She would only be able to help you reach your destination, once you tell her where you want to go. She will make all the requisite arrangements for your flight, stay, food etc after knowing your destination. That lady is analogous to our mind, which once shown a direction, will automatically find out pathways and processes to reach the destination.

There was a study done by a group of Business schools, on the students who had left college ten years ago. They were surveyed on their goals. 83% of those who polled said they were busy with their work commitments and work schedules and that they didn't find time to set goals for themselves nor were they planning to set any goals for their future. The other 14% who polled said a "yes" to setting work goals but they didn't have the habit of writing them down. And the study revealed some interesting results – the 14% of people who had set goals but didn't write them down were earning on an average, two times more than the other 83% who didn't set any goals. What about the remaining 3% people surveyed? These were the ones who were setting goals for themselves and also writing them down. And finally the most astonishing result of the study came – these 3% people on an average were the elite folks and were earning a breath taking ten times more than the other 93% people put together. Will you still like to decide whether you wish to set goals or not.

Quality of your Life will be determined by the quality of Goals you set for yourself.

Set Goals or become Tadpoles

"If you don't design your own life plan, chances are you'll fall into someone else's plan. And guess what they have planned for you? Not much."

Jim Rohn

I am convincingly sure of the fact that you did plan your vacations on a regular basis. You do not plan the place you like to go to when you get in your car, you would obviously not say "Hey baby lets go to where our car takes us". You did plan the cell phone chip you would like to have for a better connection, and you do plan the hang out place you like to meet your girlfriend. You plan so many things on a daily basis, moment by moment, but do you sit down for a minute and plan your future, a plan of where you want to reach, where are you heading to. It is an irony that we are so busy in planning so many things of our lives yet we forget to plan our future. Our World is no less than an African Jungle, where competition takes the place almost everywhere. It is a place where either you define your future or your future is defined by someone else. The famous saying goes –

"Every morning in Africa, a gazelle wakes up. It knows that it must outrun the fastest lion or it will be eaten. Every morning in Africa, a lion wakes up. It knows that it must outrun the slowest gazelle or it will starve to death. It doesn't matter whether you are a lion or a gazelle; when sun comes up you did better be running."

So, whether you are a gazelle or a lion; it doesn't matter at all, whether you are rich or poor, able or specially-abled, small or big, young or old, it doesn't matter at all – what really creates a difference is whether you are driven by your goals or by your circumstances. The time you do plan not set goals is the time you are at a mercy of your competition and the world. They will drive you in almost every aspect of your life – career, education, job and even your relationships.

Don't be a tadpole. Tadpoles are small insect like species which stay in the water and live off algae. They never make it to the adult stage, a stage developed by amphibians to ensure that only the strongest animals survive. They live off on what they find around themselves, and if they don't find anything to eat they die. Hence they are driven by their circumstances and choose to remain in the same condition throughout. Goals are lifelines, which give you the power to change your outcomes and live an amazing life full of abundance of all kinds.

Not having a goal is like being tied to the last seat of your car, and your life is taking you for a ride where ever it wants to – directionless. Hence, to take complete control of your driver seat and direct your life to the place you crave to go, find a Goal.

Man without a Goal is like a Car without a Steering, very risky and very dangerous.

A good story has its own Glory

"Take the first step in faith. You don't have to see the whole staircase, just take the first step."

Martin Luther King, Jr.

Neil Armstrong landed on the moon from the space shuttle which carried him all the way to his ultimate destination and he said, "One small step for man; one giant leap for mankind." His glory still remains because he had set the most promising examples in the history of human achievement. His message was not a message for the Americans, but a message for the World; it was a message of hope and human spirit. One small step when taken can begin the process of transforming the human history. Bill Gates took one small step with launching a computer firm named Microsoft in his garage, rest is history. Mahatma Gandhi took one step for the independence of the nation and he was followed by millions. Mother Teresa took a small step in helping the poor and underprivileged and she was bestowed with a Nobel. Michael Jordan took a small step in the basketball ground and he was crowned the best ever player in basketball history. Every human success has its origin in the modest first beginning, small yet powerful.

You have taken the first step in the process of achieving your Goal by reading this Book. That is the first step, which really means that you have accomplished 50% of your goal right away. That sounds pretty cool and yes it is, but the time you reach the end of this chapter, you will also be amazed to know what constitutes the other fifty percent – The answer to the other fifty percent lies in profound questions on Goal setting – What motivates You?; Why do you Act the way you Act?; Which is the most harmonious way to complete the Journey towards your Goal?

There are in total six basic aspects of our lives – Intellectual, Relationships, Emotional, Spiritual, Financial and Health. These are the wide spheres which govern our lives. Without each of them, your life cannot become truly satisfying. What are you doing and not doing in each of the spheres is directly affecting the quality of results you are getting, because these spheres of life are inter-related, dependent on each other. If you are emotionally well off then there is a high probability that you will be healthy in your Relationships as well. If you are spiritually balancing yourself, your intellectual capabilities are positively affected. You work on your health and you will see the results at both emotional and spiritual levels. Intellectual goals can help you reach your financial goals. These aspects of your life are weaved into one cloth and that cloth is your life. To improve every aspect of your life you need to find out how much are you faring in each aspect.

The first step in the process of getting committed to a Goal is *deciding your Goal*. Once you get to know the aspect which needs significant change, begin the process of focusing all your energies on that aspect. Decide a financial goal, a physical goal, a relationship goal, an intellectual goal, a career goal or a spiritual goal.

Setting a Goal is half the distance travelled – unsuccessful people fail to travel this half.

How to Goal a Goal?

"Man is a goal seeking animal. His life only has meaning if he is reaching out and striving for his goals."

Aristotle

How would you like a goal which says "I want to be happy". This is a goal which tells you what kind of a feeling you desire – the feeling of happiness. But it gives no specific direction you need to follow, it gives no clues as to how you will gauge your progress, it doesn't tell you what actions you need to take and in which aspect of your life; it doesn't tell you the resources you would need on the journey to achieve the goal. The first learning in setting goals is to recognize your goal in specific and clear terms.

Instead of saying "I want to lose weight" mention how much weight you like to lose. Being specific gives you a target to be achieved. Without a target success point, you are running a race with no end point; you keep on running without knowing how much more time is left, how much energy to expend and how much distance to be covered. Running such a race will give us no motivation to move forward and achieve – it is like being stagnant in life. Do we know one of the most renowned space organizations in the World has been NASA, and reason why their projects in space exploration are so successful is that they are just too specific. In most of their missions, they time their landing with precision, the point of touch, the opening and closing of fire boosters everything from ignition to touchdown is done with high precision. They know exactly the location to be landed on, the specific time when they would like the spacecraft to land and many other specifications which make it easy for them to achieve, because they know how much to achieve, where is the target, what is the outcome.

A wise man said that the things which cannot be measured cannot be achieved. There is a difference when I say I want *two glasses* full of milk and when I say I want *some* milk. *Some* can range from one drop to 1000 gallons – but what is the limit? In my seminars I ask people what is their goal and most of them will say they want Money and then my second question says, "How much money do you want", and they say "I want more money." I say to them that their wish is granted right here – I put my hands in the pocket, search for the purse and hand them a one rupee coin. Now I believe they have some money. Then they will say, we want much more than that. I look out for my purse and hand them a ten rupee note which is a thousand percent more than they got the first time. Then again I ask them "Are you happy now?" Finally getting furious over my remarks they will reply with what they really want and give out specific answers – "I want one million dollars", "I desire to earn ten thousand a day", "I long for having a thirty billion dollars in my bank account". And now that is what I call as being precisely specific.

If we observe our needs and wants in which we are not specific, we can detect two reactions. The first one being that we are never satisfied with what we get until we know how much we want and secondly if we don't get what we want at the first instance we begin to feel demotivated, because we are not sure how much will pacify us. Now when one says I want a place to stay and he gets a small house, he says he wants a bigger one. When he shifts to a bigger one, now he wants even a bigger house. It is only because of the reason he has not set a specific goal to achieve and hence the dis-satisfaction. A goal like – "I am committed to getting a house which is spread across 3 acres, with seven palatial rooms, two jacuzzis, a big lawn and a vegetable garden and a beautifully crafted Olympic size swimming pool". Now such a goal really gives a motivation.

Not being specific, is like traveling on a highway and not knowing which turn to take, whether the first one or the second one. It is same with Goal setting, where it is becomes essential to gauge your progress from moment to moment. What is your location, how much more to travel and where and when to turn to a new path. One should know the progress one makes in the process of achieving the Goal. If I say I wish to lose ten kgs of weight and I am working towards this goal, I should be able to tell any one how much progress I have made in a day, a week, a month or an year. My weight will tell me where I am right now and how much more to work for my Goal. And it will also tell me what new pathways to take if I am not making any progress. This way I am motivated to move towards my Goal. Even mountaineers follow the same process of Goal Measurement, by setting up base camps all the way to the mountain top. They reach a base camp and see how much they have progressed, at what altitude they are, what are the oxygen levels and if there is anything more they would be needing to fasten the progress, they are quick to take action.

Our lifestyle has conditioned us such that we are always in a state of want. We keep on wanting – the – want, thereby losing the power of achieving success. When we say we want something, we actually mean we are fine if we get it and if we don't get it even then we are fine. “Want” doesn't develop a sense of urgency, a sense of power in your body to achieve the goal. Another word which does not command power is “Like”. You move across the road and you see a beautiful black Toyota Camry parked in front of the road, and you say to yourself, “I like this car”. What you are actually doing is stating a preference. A better word can be “Destined”, because it brings a sense of conviction in your goal statement. Let us take an example of two different people, one says “I like to be Rich” and the other says “I am destined to be Rich” I hope you would note the difference – I changed a single word in the statement and it had a profound effect on the meaning of the statement. When the first person says he “likes” to be rich, he actually means to say that he would prefer being rich someday. Because the word “like” does not create a sense of power and influence on him. Whereas the word “Destined” creates a sense of urgency, a sense of devotion and a powerful command to the body about the goal you had set for yourself.

Examples:

See how a change in the word brings in a sense of commitment and energy

From:

“I want to lose 10kgs of weight”

“I like to earn Rs 85000 a month”

"I want a Honda with tinted black glasses and silver alloys"

"I like a house at Kensington Palace Gardens, London"

To:

"I am destined to lose 10kgs of weight within next three months"

"I am destined to earn Rs 85000 a month"

"I am destined to own Honda with tinted black glasses and silver alloys"

"I am destined to purchase a house at Kensington Palace Gardens, London"

Saying the goal statements mentally enhances the level of confidence to achieve the goal.

A clear picture like a clear goal looks lot more attractive, both to the photographer and the Goal Setter.

Priming a goal with your Timing

"If you have built castles in the air, your work need not be lost; that is where they should be. Now put the foundations under them."

Henry David Thoreau

When I joined the local gym near my house, my first day was very exciting. I had never seen such big dumbbells which weighed upto 50 kgs. They were massive to the hilt, and I thought how anyone could exercise with such heavy weights.

I asked the coach how I would progress in the gym if I do regular exercises. He said, "When a person joins a gym, he should not start exercising with the heavy weights straightaway because then he will be setting unrealistic expectations from himself which will not be met. Because either he will stress out himself or will lose the motivation. It would be like using all your energy in one go and leaving nothing for the journey. Hence setting realistic targets is what makes a good body builder". But the question that came to my mind was how I could find that realistic target. He answered, "Lift as much as you can and a little more". This piece of wisdom changed my life in a big way, because it gave me a reference point to strive for my goals. The sentence contained tons of wisdom for goal setters – start with setting a goal which is realistic and which is a little beyond your reach. Setting unrealistic goals can affect your motivation and that is the precise reason why we see so many people leave the gym after one or two months of hard work – they have expended all their energies in a very short period of time, leaving them with nothing for the rest of the Journey.

Setting too easy goals are also not useful. When the requisite skills are available and the target is well in reach, there would be no growth. Growth takes place only when we are stretched. And we also know that to reach beyond our potential is to reach the ultimate treasures of our lives. How can you expect to grow your muscles when the only weights you are lifting are those small 1kg dumbbells? Unless and until your goal is a little more than what you can achieve, growth will not take place – you remain at the same place where you were, and when you remain at the place you were, you will not be able to move to the place where you want to be. Hence always remember "Lift as much as you can and a little more".

Recall the time when you met your old friend in a mall or a market or some hang-out place. You had a little chit-chat and then what did you say to each other as you were about to leave. Remember! "We will meet someday then". I also remember a time when in my school days, I would ask my friend for an assignment and he used to say "I will provide you with the assignment in sometime". And the reality is, that someday and sometime never came. In our regular conversations we use two interesting words someday and sometime, which never come, rather they mean – no day and no time. If someone says to you we will chat someday, or we will meet someday, or we will have a discussion someday, will have a coffee sometime, and will go on a holiday sometime-they simply mean to say "just forget it". Setting a target completion date is making the goal realistic and time bound. Having a goal like "I like to earn $8000 per month someday", gives us no sense of responsibility about our goal. You are still the same as you were the next day, when you have a goal like this. And when you say, "I am destined to earn $8000 per month by February 2011", you can tell where you were yesterday and today and where will your goal stand in terms of your growth. Each day becomes significant in terms of the progress you have made. Setting a target completion date is like setting a reference point, for you to measure your goal. You give a strong message to your mind to accomplish your goal, which automatically develops the drive and commitment to make your goal a reality.

From:

"I like to lose 10kgs of weight"

"I like to earn Rs 85000 a month"

To:

"I am destined to lose 10kgs of weight by the end of September 2010"

"I am destined to earn $85000 a month by June 2011"

We have much to learn from athletes, who compete in the Olympics they prepare themselves throughout the year to break records and earn the podium. In practice, if an Olympic runner targets a time of 60 seconds, he does not aim at 60 seconds right away, rather he aims at a time of somewhere 70 – 80 seconds. With every practice he sets a new Goal for himself which will make him move closer to his aim of 60 seconds. He moves step by step the whole year to reach the landmark 60 seconds timing. That is the way Goals are set, you set sub-goals which will brighten your chance with every small win. Sub-goals can be weekly, monthly and half-yearly (intentionally not including yearly Goals for beginners) which you accomplish, and then target a new sub-goal, and then a new, until a time when these collections of small wins give you a big win at last. More the small wins, better the chance of a big win.

A bomb timer and a goal timer have a common purpose – to move people into action.

Pick the Pace and Win the Race

"There is one quality which one must possess to win, and that is definiteness of purpose, the knowledge of what one wants, and a burning desire to possess it."

Napoleon Hill

After being decisive on the goal, you would need the right resources to get through your journey. When you plan to go for a picnic, you check out the travel books, search the Internet, take reviews of people who have already visited the place, make a financial budget, search of the mode of communication – whether it will be a rail, bus, air journey etc and finally get your bookings done to the destination and hence embark on the journey. All these resources which make your journey possible are your preparatory guide to reach the goal.

Resources give power to drive you towards your Target; they act as a rope to the one who is flowing in tough currents. Resources can be many – financial, people, knowledge, experience etc.

Having an inventory of the resources you will need to accomplish your Goals, will do a great help to you in making your journey harmonious and focused. This is a comprehensive resource planning list which will act as a guide for you in your journey –

1. People (including the ones who are experienced, experts in the fields concerned you're your Goal)

2. Written Material (Books, Magazines, Journals, Articles or any other written document)

3. Financial Resources (how will you create the resources if they are not sufficient)

4. Internet (forums, groups, chat rooms, websites and other online resources)

5. Friends and Family (who would assist you in acquiring the skills you will need to achieve)

For hitting your target you will need certain skills that will help you achieve your Goal. For example, you may have the right talent for playing cricket, but for getting into the School cricket team, you would be needing skills such as Consistency and Persistence or you may have to learn to Market yourself better to your Coach. If you have not achieved your Goal that simply means you need the right skill to bridge the gap between your present state and your achievement state.

STORY OF MILO-The Muscle Man

There was a man named Milo born in Croton, somewhere in Italy. He went on to become six time champion at the Greek Olympics. He won championships because he used the formula of success – goal setting. This man in his childhood would carry a calf on his shoulders and walk. As he grew so did the calf, but still he used to carry the calf long distances knowing that the weight of the calf was also increasing. He knew that at some time he will be able to develop massive strength once he is able to lift a complete bull. And he persisted in carrying the calf till it became a bull, on a daily basis. Slow daily effort began to reap results when he grew up to become an adult. His persistence use of resources available to him made him into a powerful man. He was able to carry a bull across one mile and due to this he built up incredible strength, power and energy that no one possessed. And henceforth we won the Olympic championships.

When all the available resources are focused towards achieving a Goal; Goal cannot help but Manifest.

Your Priorities determine Your Outcome

"If you go to work on your goals, your goals will go to work on you. If you go to work on your plan, your plan will go to work on you. Whatever good things we build end up building us."

Jim Rohn

The Pareto's principle has taught us much beyond the wealth distribution, which it talked about. Vilfredo Pareto found out in 1906 that 80% of the land in Italy was owned by 20% of the population. He also tried to find out mathematical solutions to economic problems. Not only that, with his experience he also observed that 20 percent of the peapods in the garden yielded 80 percent of the peas that were harvested. That was the origin of the much accepted 80/20 Rule, which was not only used in business but also in Life management too.

Some people have also found out some interesting facts after the acceptance of this principle:

20% of your dresses in the closet are worn 80% of the time

20% of the car (engine) gives 80% drive

20% of your friends account for 80% of your enjoyment

20% of the clients in a business give you 80% of the Revenues

20% of the employees are responsible for 80% of the Business in a company

In Life management too, 20% of your activities determine 80% of the outcomes you get. Being too much occupied in doing things which do not produce meaningful results reduce your ability to deliver. It is a shift which needs to be brought from focus on doables to deliverables. One of the best ways to find out those 20% activities is to question the outcome of action you take. Is the outcome in line with your Goal? Will it help you in anyway reach the goal you have wished for? If it is not, move away from the action and focus your energies on the activity which creates a difference. Most of the time people focus their attention on petty matters which are out of alignment or are not at all related to their greatest priorities and goals, without knowing what outcome they desire, they are driven by their busy schedules, so that they can keep busy and satisfy their inner being consistently showcasing that they are the busiest people on the planet.

Where as a leader will always chose the outcome first and then devise the activity he should be engaged into. Asking yourself this question – "What is the outcome of my action and is the outcome in line with my Goal?" should be your litmus test for ascertaining your priorities. Have you not seen people who remain busy almost all the time, and then when the time comes, there are no outcomes. And then they say "That is not my cup of tea". And yes they are true because it is not their cup of tea to find purposes to their actions and thoughts; rather they are driven by circumstances and not by their will.

The next question that comes to my mind is how to determine those activities which help you move towards your goal, which activity will produce maximum result for you to get closer to your outcome? List down all the activities you do or would do to reach your goal. Think of as many things as you can – look out for all the resources and actions which you believe will add value to yourself and will move you from your current state to your future state. Challenge for you is to rank those items (actions and resources) according to the outcomes – most significant outcome which will add maximum value ranks one, second significant outcome ranks second and so on, do this exercise for all the activities. In the end you will have a rank wise activity/action list, which will help you determine your priorities. Take the top 20% of the items and you will have the 20% of your activities which will give you 80% of the results in your life.

Go into the World and enjoy the game. You have the target, you have the resources, and you know what to do, how much better life can become.

This list of actions are then placed according to the time they would take to reap results in the goal setting sheet. For every action write down the outcome you desire from it. The outcome will define in specific terms what will happen when you take action. The last column will give you the time for which the action will be taken or the time limit when the action will start reaping results. When you put a time limit, you create a momentum in your actions which helps you gauge your progress on a daily basis. You would know how much to achieve, by how much time and the amount of energies to be put in for making you move faster in getting desired outcome, thereby reducing the incubation time for you to get results.

My action item list for my __________ Goal

My Top 20% Actions	Outcome	When will it reap the results/Time limit to you Outcome
Action 1	Detailed outcome of the action you take – What is the end result	Weekly/Monthly/Half Yearly/Yearly
Action 2	Detailed outcome of the action you take – What is the end result	Weekly/Monthly/Half Yearly/ Yearly
Action 3	Detailed outcome of the action you take – What is the end result	Weekly/Monthly/Half Yearly/ Yearly
Action 4	Detailed outcome of the action you take – What is the end result	Weekly/Monthly/Half Yearly/ Yearly
Action 5	Detailed outcome of the action you take – What is the end result	Weekly/Monthly/Half Yearly/ Yearly

My action item list for my Financial Goal

My Top 20% Actions	Outcome	When will it reap the results/Time limit to you Outcome
Sell my product/service to as many people as possible	Increased reach and penetration of my product/service. The minimum number of selling to be done is 500 units.	6 months (Jan – June)
Read top 10 sales book	To acquire insights into the selling process, and gain mastery over practicing those skills when I sell and making a note of best practices.	2 months (Jan – Feb)
To meet five new people who would benefit from my product/service	Develop a network of people who would be a future prospect to my business. 5 new people to be added to the network per day.	Daily
Find as many uses of my product/service	To develop new markets for my product/service apart from the regular use.	1 month (Jan)
Market my product/service at exhibition	Increased visibility of my product/service and making people aware about them. To market my product/service at the International Trade Fair, Auto Fair, CII Conference etc.	1 year (Jan – Dec)

All your actions, thoughts and emotions are directed towards an imaginary circle which represents the kind of results you will get in your life. This is called the "Circle of Results". Such a circle acts as a compass for us to direct our actions to the results we want in our life. This circle comprises of two areas – the inner circle and the outer circle – inner circle represents the area of your Influence and the outer circle is the "out of bounds" area. The successful and the unsuccessful people have a unique distinction in the way they take action, which results in getting the outcome they desire. The ones who direct their thoughts, actions and feelings towards those areas which help them reach their Goal are the ones who make progress in their journey, unlike the ones who do not make significant progress and focus their energies on the Out of Bounds area without any outcome. A person of this type would say, "I want people to love me", "I want others to change their behavior", "I want him to take up this initiative", "I would like her to talk with the management". Such statements give him no power to change his circumstances because he has placed the responsibility of action on others. While the successful person would say, "I will love people so that they start to love me", "I would like to change my behavior before I expect others to change", "I would like to take up this initiative and would like people to join me then", "I will go and talk with the Managers to explain my problems." Such responsible statements clearly put the onus of action on him rather than putting the responsibility on other people. Such a successful man would always take control of his destiny and steer his life in the direction he wants. It is a simple principle which made the distinction between these two people, which says that when the focus of one's actions changes from the "Out of Bounds" area to the "Circle of Influence" one begins to take direct control of his life and results he desired.

Let me ask you a question – can you control the weather, temperature, the frequency of rainfall, what people think in their minds, how your friends talk and behave or the quality of a nation's GDP. Only when you have an extra-ordinary ability you can change all these variables, but in reality it is way too difficult. Now tell me, do you have a control over what you will wear on a particular day, what will you think in your mind, what will you say when you meet an old friend, the way you will improve your financial condition. I must say compared to the previous list we stand a better chance of controlling these internal variables which are affected by the actions directly.

When you begin to take actions which are affecting your internal variables you stand a much better chance of changing your life. Imagine the time when you felt bad about what your friend said to you, you felt totally disgruntled and angry, end result of such a focus on what he said, depleted all your energy and hence made your day, week, month or a year hell, only by thinking of what you couldn't control directly. Now if you had thought about the Circle of Results, you would have focused your actions, thoughts and feelings on what you can control i.e. your behavior, conduct, response. You have the power to alter your attitude instantaneously after such an incident and free yourself from the clutches of Negativity. That is the choice we have but only when we begin to appreciate and use the Circle of Results we begin to see powerful results with our actions.

There is a difference between a hard-worker who is successful and the hard-worker who is unsuccessful. The hard-worker who is unsuccessful will keep his Thoughts, Actions and Feelings on the "Out of Bounds" area and hence would not get meaningful results, because his focus is on activities which are simply not in his control. The successful hard-worker will direct his actions to those activities which are directly affected by his actions, because he has learnt to differentiate between what he can control and what he cannot and hence he has the direction and target to concentrate his actions to a limited set of meaningful areas.

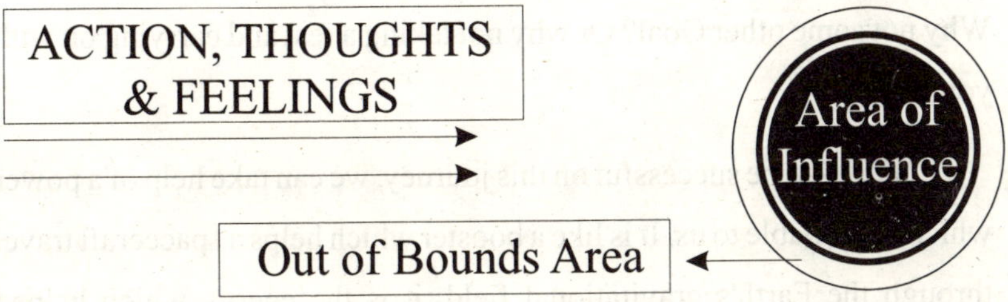

Fig: The Circle of Results

My actions today will determine where I will arrive tomorrow – act today and accomplish tomorrow.

The Why of your Motivation

"Whatever the mind can conceive and believe it can achieve."

Napoleon Hill

Why do you want to have a Goal you have decided for yourself? Why not some other Goal? Or why not taking a rest and carrying on with your Life?

For us to be successful on this journey, we can take help of a power which is available to us. It is like a booster which helps a spacecraft travel through the Earth's gravitational field, it is the energy which helped people like Mahatma Gandhi, Abraham Lincoln, Bill Gates, Steve Jobs and many others Leaders of the World become amazingly successful. It is the Power of Emotions – we can tap into this power if we know the precise reason we are following a Goal or a Target. Knowing the "why" of a goal is eighty percent success, and knowing the "how" is just twenty percent of your Success. Driving force behind high powered achievement and peak performances is Emotions. Once we are aware of our emotions we will be empowered to bring out the motivation needed to get results from our actions. E.g. I want to get rid of this illness because I desire to have a *feeling of vivacity*, I am destined to evolve this relationship because I have a desire to *feel love.* What is driving you to attain the goal, what is the feeling you like to address when you have reached the goal?

Challenge for us is to recognize those inherent feelings which drive us towards our needs and wants. Like every tree stands on the ground because of its roots, similarly every desire of yours has its roots in your Emotions or Feelings. Once we know what drives the root of our want – what are the deep rooted emotions we need to address, we can water the root and grow fruits on our tree as we desire.

Let us find out how our feelings are associated with our thoughts. Our mind does not think in words, it understands in pictures, sounds and feelings. When I ask you to think about a Black Porsche – what you will think about will be a picture associated with this car in your mind, and if you have not seen the car, chances are that you will recall the feelings associated with this car that is luxury, comfort, power etc or your may recall what someone said to you about this car and will recall the voices from inside your mind. It has been scientifically and biologically proven fact that we are emotionally moved only because of our interpretation of reality which happens through three powerful channels – Visual, Auditory and Feelings. In Goal setting it becomes essential for us to recognize this fact and use it to our advantage as much as possible. What do we see when we have achieved this Goal? What would I hear from my family, friends, colleagues and other people? Most importantly how would I feel when I accomplish my Goal? Visualizing this Goal in these three aspects can change the way you act on a daily basis – see what you will see, hear what you will hear and feel what you will feel, but do it Now.

I. What would I *see* when I have achieved my Goal

II. What sounds, conversations, talks, voices would I *hear* when I have achieved my Goal

III. What would be the *feelings* I would feel when I have reached my Goal

Answering these questions will bring you to a point, where you will begin to see yourself in the emotion which you desire. For example a boy has a goal of having a loving relationship with his partner. He sees himself been hugged by his partner sitting on a red couch, he listens to the background soft music being played, the winds blowing softly, and feels the emotion of being cared and loved, a feeling of being secure. All these three aspects, combine and make him realize what he wants, how much he wants, how does he want it, where does he want it, when does he like to manifest it. On repeating this exercise he waters the emotion which is driving him towards his ultimate desire. And this makes him stay on the path of his desire, it defines his daily choices and he doesn't forget his ultimate goal of having loving relationships. More often than not, the failure to achieve a goal is attributed to fact that humans have a tendency of forgetting their desires. When we were children, we knew what happiness was – we were happy even on sunset, when our friend used to come at our home, we were happy to see the policeman with a whistle in his mouth, but as we grow older, we tend to forget what brings us happiness, we don't feel happy on sunset, we have no time to spend with our loved ones and rather than being happy seeing a policeman, we think of getting away from him. The reason for this is not that we don't have goals, but we tend to forget our goals as we move on with our lives. Remaining in the emotion, keeps the light of your goal burning.

It is said that every event in your life happens twice – once in the mind and then in the real world. It is like having a mental rehearsal of your goal, before it happens in reality. If you wish to manifest your goal in reality, begin seeing, hearing and feeling it in your mind and you will very soon be seeing, hearing and feeling it in the real world. Someone said – "Losers visualize the penalties of failure. Winners visualize the rewards of success."

See, Hear and Feel your success and you will accomplish your Goal with finesse.

Why don't you become an Addict?

"The tragedy of life doesn t lie in not reaching your goal. The tragedy lies in having no goals to reach."

Benjamin Mays

Dictionary.com defines addiction as "The state of being enslaved to a habit or practice or to something that is psychologically or physically habit-forming".

We in the course of our lifetime have been addicted to so many things – and mostly to the things which were transient, which were not ours. As a child we were addicted to our G.I Joes, Mickey Mouses, Donald Ducks, and Cartoon Television; when we grew older and reached the teens stage we were addicted to our girlfriends or boyfriends, we were addicted to the feeling of love, we were addicted to our games – basketball, volleyball, cricket etc. And now when we step into adulthood, we again get addicted to all kinds drugs, cigarettes, drinks and last but not the least money. We have been addicted to things which were never ours.

I would like you to become-an addict an addict of something which you own yourself – your own Goals. It is the only addiction which will be with you every day, hour, minute and second. Benefits are amazing when addiction becomes intense – you go beyond yourself to satisfy the need and the best part is results start flowing in.

Haven't you heard of Goal Addicts of this World – the teenagers who had a goal of organizing the World's information and make it accessible to all – Google, a single mother who had a goal to write a book, became a millionaire within no time – J K Rowling, a small 14 year old boy found an addiction in a goal to become a body builder, who then went on to become Mr. Olympia a total of seven times – Arnold Schwarzenegger. All of them from J K Rowling to Arnold Schwarzenegger and from Larry Page and Sergey Brin to Steve Jobs and Bill Gates were Goal Addicts. They were passionate about their invisible dreams in their minds, and they made them visible in reality by following their own road map, their own chart of Goals. The only thing they cared about was that there should not be a goal scarcity in their lives. They lived on goals – short term and long term, daily to yearly goals, always planning where they have to go next, what is their next pit stop. A goal brings action in their lives, bringing with it the excitement, energy, passion, love and an unconquerable will to live their purpose.

A good way to remember the importance of setting goals, is to become an addict, and think of goal setting process as a drug. The more pleasure you get from completing your Goals (the satisfaction that comes from achieving realistic, challenging goals), the more you would like to set up goals. Once you get comfortable with the process, you will be doing more of it. And why should not you-It will help you achieve anything you want in all aspects of your life – Financial, Personal, Relationships, Academics, Work, Physical, Emotional Goals. It's just like a catalogue you have been offered by someone divine – you choose and define what you want, and you will get everything of it.

Addict yourself to setting and accomplishing goals, and soon you will realize that you are living a life you dreamt once.

Your Motivation, Your Emotions, Your Power

Who are we! What you see on the outside is just the matter, which is getting old every moment; it is degenerating at a pace that you don't seem to know. But there is another "You", which lies inside the body, which is the soul, it is the life giving energy and is unlimited in quantity. This energy gives us the ultimate power which makes us different from machines – it is the power of Emotions. As the lion wields its power through physical force, in the same manner this life giving energy wields its power through the force of Emotions. Channelizing emotions towards a particular task can make breakthroughs happen, revolutionalize human potential and make people move from good to great to phenomenal. I challenge you to make use of this unlimited resource.

Know how to attain Sustainable Success

"There can be no transforming of darkness into light and of apathy into movement without emotion."

Carl Gustav Jung

Throughout the day, you go through millions of emotions that drive how you feel in your body. Emotions can be of many types – Happiness, Enthusiasm, Apathy, Empathy, Sadness, Distressful, Excitement, Passion, Love, Care, Sympathy, Boredom, Bravery, Stubbornness, Thankfulness, Dullness, Loneliness, Anxiety, Fear, and many more. We have gone through each of them at least thousands of times in our lives and they affect us in different ways – some emotions are painful and some bring us joy or from what I see they are either Resourceful or Non-Resourceful. Each feeling will define how you feel inside the body and how you act in the external environment. You may have experienced a situation where you are feeling annoyed and then someone comes up with his/her problem and you say, "Shut up! Don't you know I am so occupied and you too have brought your worries to me." It is because our internal emotions drive our responses on a daily basis.

We are always in a State of some emotion and hence that emotion drives us every moment. Even now when you read this literature, you are in a state of concentration.

Ask yourself what kind of emotions you feel on a daily basis and

BRUCE WILLIS- Conqueror of Fear

We have grown up watching his movies, be it Armageddon – where he saves the World with wit and compassion or the Die Hard series where he takes on the enemies of state and shows the real action he possesses. What we do not know about this great man is that he overcame a significant childhood challenge which would have severed his chances of making it to Hollywood. He faced a challenge of stuttering when he was in his college days, which he overcame very soon when he observed something miraculous about his ability. He noticed that when he went on stage he was a completely different person delivering a perfect intonation and with fluency, than when he was in a normal state. He said in an interview with a magazine that, "The key to it was the fact that when I got onstage and when I was an actor, I didn't stutter. That was a miracle in itself." This actor went into completely different state which empowered him to conquer his disability – it is because he used the power of resourceful emotional state which he used whenever he went on stage.

make a list of the emotions you experience throughout the day. After you have known the emotions you feel on a daily basis, you would also know that some emotions help you perform better and some make you go low on energy.

Differentiate between empowering and dis-empowering emotions, which you have listed. Why I am saying this is because , there are certain kinds of emotions that we will not be comfortable experiencing as they lower our productivity, divert our attention, make us feel less powerful and sap our energy. Difference between successful and unsuccessful, haves and have-nots, winners and losers is the amount of time they spend in an empowering state. You would have seen that the Go-Getters of life are inclined towards emotions like excitement, passion, energy and similar kinds of empowering emotional states, whereas the unsuccessful people spend most of their life in negative dis-empowering states like gloominess, unexcited, monotonous, tired etc.

Our States define the way we deliver results. For example, in cricket what do we mean when selectors say that the player is in form or out of form? They mean that the player is in a successful state which makes him perform better on a consistent basis and moreover he has a greater chance of replicating his excellent performance in the next coming matches which he plays. A state is a set of *physiological* – related to body, *emotional* – empowering or dis-empowering emotions, and *mental* conditions – the content and attitude of your mind, which when combined together at a particular instant, makes it possible for you to get results. But before we begin the process of replicating powerful states to form a pattern of brilliance in our life, we have to be aware of our states. What are your positive and negative states, what are the emotions which occupy your mind and body and keep you misaligned? Awareness brings a new light in the dark, where we search for our peak performance.

List all your States/Emotions into Resourceful and Un-Resourceful states categories. Few examples of Powerful states are – Passion, Confidence, Fluency, Congruency, Positivity, Empathy, Love, Care, Compassion, Charm, Elegance, Assured, Transcendent, Peaceful, Glory, Adventure, Sublime, Glamour, Grace, Secure, Balanced, Brave, Grounded, Delightful, Pleased, Elated, Thrilled, Humor, Proud, Assured and many more.

Examples of Un-Resourceful States may be – Dejection, Ashamed, Condemned, Dismal, Gloomy, Disgrace, Remorse, Scared,

Insecure, Sunken, Abandoned, Hollow, Depresses, Nervous, Fear, Shy, Humiliated, Pathetic, Timid, Left out and many more.

Complete the list with the Resourceful states which you like to repeat in your daily lives and the Un-Resourceful states which you like to get rid off in your life.

Resourceful States	Un-Resourceful States

After this exercise you have made yourself clear which of your states give you pleasure and pain, which you want and which you don't want, which give you power and which dis-empowers you.

But the biggest question that comes to our mind is that when we know our empowering and de-empowering states why we don't replicate those states when needed. For example, you felt confident while giving a presentation once, but the next time you gave the presentation you were not able to replicate the same confidence in your body, you lacked the emotion of power and influence, and your body didn't communicate well when you spoke. Even when you assume that there is no change in your preparation or environment variables, even then you will agree that we are inept to replicate most of our best performances. Have we not seen sportsmen who could not continue to be in a state of winning on a consistent basis, while a few top class sportsmen retaining their championship belt year on year. The reason behind those successful sportsmen breaking records year on year, winning championship year on year, is that they are not only aware of their resourceful states but also know how to be in that state for longer periods.

State is a combination of physiological, emotional and mental conditions which combine at a particular instant to empower you to deliver results – good and bad both.

Master your Life using this

"Anchoring is the most effective technique I know for constructively channeling our powerful unconscious reactions so they are always at our disposal. It s a way to ensure that we always have access to our greatest resources."

Tony Robbins

When you cross a particular place, there are certain kinds of feelings that originate in your mind and body, when you open your old gifts you feel the same emotions which you felt when you opened them for the first time, when you come across a peculiar smell, it reminds you of something, a touch which may bring back memories of some past emotion, watching a movie you listen to a type of music and you know that the hero of the movie is about to arrive.

There was man named Rick, who was a regular visitor of a local temple. But after the funeral of his wife near the temple, he was not able to return to the temple again. There were certain feelings associated with the place which brought a sense of grief to him after the death of his wife. Hence an emotion and a place combined together was a signal for him to experience the state of pain.

Sometimes words like "Sex" can cause some images to trigger in your mind and cause some intense emotion in your body; the word "Money" can fire yet another emotion of feeling wealthy, successful, luxury etc. We are been exposed to so many commercials through Television, Radio, Posters and many other sources, and if you examine those commercials carefully, you will observe that they are actually not selling a product or an equipment or a service, they are selling what I say is an emotion, through their product which is an anchor. See the advertisement of BMW and they have associated a feeling of "Luxury" with it; Apple has associated their products with a feeling of being "Innovative"; Maruti has associated their product with a feeling of "Economy". This explains how we get motivated or feel positively when we buy a product. This process of associating an emotion to a stimulus, so that when the stimulus gets fired, it brings with it the emotion associated with it to the person, is called Anchoring and the stimulus is called an Anchor.

Emotion + Stimuli→ Successful Anchor

Anchors are stimuli which call forth a state of mind – thoughts and emotions. Anchors are generally subconsciously set in the minds of people, without them knowing about it. Example, smell as an anchor which reproduces certain past feelings, passing across a particular road sign serves as an anchor to make us feel certain types of emotions, and in the example of Rick, going to the temple acts as an anchor which brings out the feeling of pain in Rick's mind as visiting the temple is associated with a feeling of grief for Rick.

The process of Anchoring had its origin in the science of achieving peak performances which is called NLP–Neuro Linguistic Programming. The concept was founded by two people, Richard Bandler and John Grinder who were engaged in the study of achieving powerful results in human performances. They gave various lectures and seminars all across the World on formulas of Success through use of mental processes using NLP concepts.

NLP is made up of three words. Neuro simply means the nervous system or the mind and refers to the how our mind works, Linguistic means the language systems we use and how it affects us, and Programming refers to the behavioral patterns we use to learn through our experiences. Anchoring as a pattern has been used in NLP to create meaningful measurable results in individuals and is a widely popular technique among the NLP practitioners. Today, anchoring is being used in every type of industry to motivate people and help them perform at extra ordinary levels. It has been used in diverse fields like sports, sales, marketing, television, movies, corporate communication, human resources etc. wherever there is need to achieve peak results.

When I take my own example, I observe that in my childhood, whenever I broke an unsaid rule of the house, my mother would call my name at the top of her voice with a completely different tone – "Nissssssssssssssssssshu" and at that point I knew I have done something wrong. Now whenever she calls me with the same kind of tonality, I did better know that I have broken a rule. It is because the way she says my name with a peculiar tone and pitch, it becomes an anchor for me which reminds me that I did get an alert of some wrong doing.

All these initiators of feelings are nothing but anchors for our mind. When an anchor is fired or is encountered, the feeling associated, originates in our body. It is just like pressing certain buttons to get a desired output.

There was a famous professor of Psychology named Edwin

Burket Twitmyers who studied the working of a human brain and its responses. He was born in McElhattan, Pennsylvania on September 14, 1873 and received his bachelor's degree from Lafayette College in 1896. He then became an Instructor in the field of Psychology and then further received a doctoral degree, after which he was appointed as a Professor at University of Pennsylvania.

He did an experiment on how humans are conditioned with certain events. He did this experiment with college students, in which he tested their knee-jerk reaction, with an alteration that he sounded a bell just half a second before he hit them on the knee. He did this test several times and he found out that even before he hit the knee and just after sounding of the bell, students reacted with a reflex. This happened because students have conditioned themselves with ringing of the bell to the feeling of being hit, and as soon as the bell rang, the students would elicit the same reflex. This study was done before Pavlov came with his breakthrough experiment on the same lines.

Pavlov studied dogs, and discovered that they would salivate upon seeing, smelling, and tasting food. He added the sound of a bell when he gave the dogs the food and after repeating the process several times he observed, he would only sound the bell to elicit their salivation response, means on hearing the ring of the bell the dogs start to salivate without the presence of food. This shows that ringing the bell was an anchor to the dogs and caused them to elicit a state of hunger.

Let us take an example of a book you are reading. Now if you find something important in the book that you would like to refer to time and again, you will bookmark that page. Now tell me how good will you feel when you know how to bookmark powerful empowering states of confidence, passion, intelligence, innovation, calmness etc. so that we may use them again and again as per our wish and begin to control our lives and our emotions rather than being living like a slave to our states. Anchoring is almost same as what Pavlov did with the dogs, i.e. associating a unique stimulus to a specific state, when you desire to have that state just trigger the stimulus or anchor and you get access to the required state instantly.

Negative States: Many of us have negative anchors as well. It is like some experience of yours which dis-empowers you. For example, take the story of a girl named Amanda. In her childhood, she was playing with a pet dog in the evening when it gave Amanda a bite on her right leg. She went into a shock, an ordeal which she had never expected. Now, when she has become an adult, she is still afraid and in a state of trauma whenever she sees a dog walking across her. It is because that childhood incident acted as an anchor for her to revoke the same experience of pain and agony. It happens almost all the time with us on a daily basis. There are certain incidents of our past which have caused us pain, and we still let them ruin our life making us filled with fear all the time. I have personally seen so many people, who are now afraid of getting into a relationship because they have associated pain with getting into a relationship, which serves as an anchor reminding them of some past pain they have experienced. They have set a relationship anchor because they had either faced a loss of a loved one, or were left out by their partners, which caused them to experience pain whenever they had a thought of getting into a relationship.

The greatest challenge of life is to destroy previous set negative anchors and create as many anchors as possible which make you experience positive states. This way you can also be successful in whatever you do and bring out new shining results in activities you engage yourself into.

> *The people who are successful remain in the Resourceful state more than the ones who are unsuccessful.*

The Magical Process – Anchoring

"Let's not forget that the little emotions are the great captains of our lives and we obey them without realizing it."

Vincent Van Gogh

1. SELECT: Select a feeling or emotion that you would like to use repeatedly in your life. Example of states may be – Confidence, Love, Passion, Energy, Calmness, Empathy, Focus and Concentration. It is a state which you like to always be in because it helps you perform better in a particular situation. Example, you need confidence before you make an official presentation hence the state desired is – Confidence; you wish to develop calmness before you attend a meeting – state desired is Calmness; you need alertness of mind while negotiating – the state required is Concentration. All these instances require you to be in a state which helps you perform at extra ordinary levels of performance. First task for you is to select the state in which you require to be in either for facing a challenge or a fear.

2. RECALL: Recall a time in your life when you had experienced that feeling. Close your eyes and remember for example a time when you felt highly confident. Choose a memory which is sharp and clear in your mind which helps you recall the state of confidence. It might happen that you could not find a state in your memory when you felt highly confident of a situation, in that case *Imagine* a time that you are feeling highly confident though it may not have occurred in real time. Why I say this is because our brain doesn't differentiate between what is real and what is imagined, a good example can be ecstasy, where our mind doesn't

differentiate between the real and the imaginary, and yet we are aroused in both states.

Questions which may help you recall the experience may be "Remember a particular time when you felt completely/fully ________ (passionate, confident, calm, intelligent etc)."; "Think of the time when you were totally ________ (feeling an emotion which you like to anchor for further use)".

When you begin go back in time and recall the state, focus as vividly as possible on the memory, as if you are experiencing right now: what would you *see* in your mind with you stepping inside your body seeing with your own eyes the people, place, your surrounding; what do you *hear* – the sounds, voices; what do you *smell* – any aroma associated with that situation; what *emotions* are you feeling in your own body.

To have a true vivid experience, focus on your memory by making the image in your mind sharp and make the colors bright, make the sounds clearer and crispier. Sometimes to make the feeling stronger in your mind, choose a word that will give you a gust of emotion – example can be "YES", "HEY", "BRILLIANT", "YA" etc. Haven't you seen football teams entering the ground with their song, or word or slogan – they are re-enforcing the emotion in their body which makes them more energetic and passionate. That is what you do to intensify the emotion.

To increase intensity

a. See the movie of your memory as clearly as possible
b. Hear the sounds which are present
c. Make the picture as bright and vivid
d. Increase the size of image in your mind

e. See from your own eyes what is happening as if you are experiencing it – associate with the memory

f. Choose words to intensify the experience. E.g. Yes, Ho, Ya etc.

3. ANCHOR: When your feeling is at its most intense stage, create a physical action by making a unique movement or gesture. For example, squeeze your thumb, close your fingers and make a fist. You may use any physical movement that you desire which is unique. I have designed a special anchor which gives me the energy I need, during my seminars. The movement of my hands vigorously towards the right serves as a kinesthetic anchor, which replenishes my energy and I am back on the track with my workshop. This is because I have anchored my hand movement to the state of energy and confidence, which I use every time I need to get into the state instantly. That is the way I use anchoring during my seminars. Make a unique gesture or movement using your body to anchor the state you want to have when the feeling of the state is at maximum. There are several movements which may be used – making a circle with your fingers, pressing your thumb on index finger, making a sign of right with your finger etc. One of the most powerful anchors which I use while I deliver my seminars is holding the mike, which I have associated with a state which delivers coherence of thoughts for me. It is an excellent way to start my seminars with clarity of thought.

Anchors can be Visual, Auditory or Kinesthetic. Visual means seeing an object for example a pen, a board, a conference hall etc. Auditory anchors are used commonly during meditation, it is just like speaking a word and you reach into a state of meditation, it is because your body has anchored a meditative state with the sound of the word. The way my mother calls my name serves as an anchor for me that I have done something wrong. Kinesthetic anchors means using a touch to develop certain types of states in the body example can be squeezing your fingers to form a fist, pressing your thumb into your index finger etc. Chose any anchor which is convenient and then fire as soon as you reach the most intense state of your feeling.

4. RELEASE: As the feeling decreases, release your anchor, i.e. if you are squeezing your thumb, loosen the squeeze and relax, if you are speaking a word, reduce the intensity, if you are viewing an object close your eyes as the feeling decrease. Purpose is to associate the anchor to the peak state only.

5. BREAK STATE: As the feeling reduces to minimum, stop and do something which is totally different. Example, say your cell number from the end to start in your mind, star counting from 20 to 1 in intervals of 2, stand up and shake your body. This will break the state and will successfully anchor the empowering emotion to the anchor you have created.

6. REPEAT: Select another memory which has given you the same state and follow the first five steps again but using the same gesture. Repeat this process with at least five different memories (remember you can always imagine if you don't get real)

SELECT-->RECALL-->ANCHOR-->RELEASE-->BREAK STATE-->REPEAT

Test your Anchor:

Fire off or use the anchor and check how powerful you feel in that State. If you want a more powerful and intense state repeat the above steps until you get the desired intensity. Everyone wants a different intensity of emotion and according to the repetition you may acquire the desired intensity. It is just like pressing the accelerator to gain more speed. The more you press, the faster you car runs and more emotional gust you experience.

Now when you need to experience a state which you have anchored you need to fire off the anchor and experience the emotions and feelings associated with your anchor.

There are four basic principles of Anchoring which can make a huge difference in developing Anchors – the UNIT approach

1. Unique: The anchor you provide for a particular state should be unique.

2. Number of repetitions: Repeat the process of setting up anchor as many times as possible with different memories (real or imaginary).

3. Intensity of emotion: Make the emotional state of feeling as intense as possible before anchoring it to the stimulus.

4. Timing: Shoot off a stimulus only when you have reached the most intense state of your emotion.

Use Anchoring to remain in Success State and you will begin to deliver results at extra ordinary levels.

The Success tool of The Century – Visualization

Training has become of prime importance today, when scope for errors has gone down to zero. Making errors could be the death knell of your business in present times of severe cut throat competition. You may be involved in decision making or handling a particular job or writing a national level exam or managing your love life or giving the most coveted job interview, the margin for errors is very less. We need a tool which can make us shine in such situations where margin of errors are sharp and when we need to run on the razor sharp blade without getting hurt showcasing incredible mental strength. The secret is buried inside our mind – it is called mental training. This secret was hidden until a time when series of experiments were done in sports psychology and the formula was discovered – the DNA to incredible performance was found in Visualization. I ask you to read more on this topic below, but more importantly I ask you to use it as you read it.

Use it to Believe it

"We are what we think. All that we are arises with our thoughts."

Buddha

Close your eyes and imagine holding a fresh cold orange in your right hand. Feel the texture, the size of the orange. As you slice it open with a knife, you see the juice oozing out of it on your fingers and palm. The aroma of orange reaches your nostrils and you feel its freshness in your body. Finally you squeeze the orange in your mouth with its fresh juice pouring on your tongue, while you feel the taste.

Did you feel the taste of orange when you did this exercise? Did you experience a sensation going through your body from your lips down to your legs? That is the power of our new pointer for success which is called Visualization.

Want to try out a more effective exercise – Close your eyes and imagine a clean blackboard in front of you. Your nails are not cut and you scratch your nails over the blackboard vigorously from the left to the right hand side of the board. And as you do it, you feel a strong sensation of your nails scratching the board, hardness on your nails as it moves.

These two exercises help us know that we don't need to be in reality to experience the feeling which we can do in the mind. This process of creating or recalling an event in the mind is being termed as Visualization.

Let us point out an experiment done by Russians at 1980 Lake Placid Olympics which gave breakthrough results in achieving Peak

Performances in sports. The scientists divided the World-Class athletes into four groups according to how they trained before the Olympics.

Group 1: 100% physical training
Group 2: 75% physical training and 25% mental training or visualization
Group 3: 50% physical training and 50% mental training or visualization
Group 4: 25% physical training and 75% mental training or visualization

After the Moscow Olympics and the Lake Placid Olympics the Performance of each group was gauged and it was found out to a surprise that Group 4 which had taken 25% physical training and 75% mental training won the most medals and showed Maximum Performance.

This event sent a message across to psychologists' community that Visualization or mind training needs to be accepted as a standard tool for achieving maximum performances. If Olympic athletes can make such a profound difference in their ability to get results, imagine how you will be able to tap into the unlimited potential of Visualization to achieve greater and bigger results on a daily basis.

Camille Duvall, an American Water-skier and a World Champion, says, "I train myself mentally with visualization. The morning of a tournament, before I put my feet on the floor, I visualize myself making perfect runs with emphasis on technique, all the way through to what my personal best is in practice.... The more you work with this type of visualization, especially when you do it on a day-to-day basis, you'll actually begin to feel your muscles contracting at the appropriate times."

Visualization makes massive difference in the capacity to deliver both motor and intellectual results for us.

The Nuts and Bolts of Mental Training

"Ordinary people believe only in the possible. Extraordinary people visualize not what is possible or probable, but rather what is impossible. And by visualizing the impossible, they begin to see it as possible."

Cherie Carter-Scott

In the 1980s, Dr. Denis Waitley used a concept which was called "Visual Motor Rehearsal" for Olympic athletes. These athletes were put sophisticated biofeedback equipments to gauge the responses of their muscles and their firing sequence. After which these Olympic athletes were asked to run the race, but ONLY in their mind. They had to fully visualize themselves in race as if it was real. The results of the experiment were path breaking. They found out that the same muscles fired as in actual race conditions and they fired in the same sequence as if the athlete is actually running the race. The big question the scientists were asking was how could the same muscles fire in the same sequence as if the athletes were running the race in reality. The answer was very clear – that our mind by default doesn't have the capability to differentiate between what is real and what is imaginary. Needless to say that Visualization holds the key to achieving Peak Performances.

The principle of Visualization lies in one abnormal biological condition of our Mind, which Dr. Denis Waitley stated as –"The mind cannot tell the difference between an actual, real-life event and a vividly imagined one".

Psychoneuromuscular theory states that Visualization rehearsals produce the similar neuromuscular responses to those of an actual experience. This means that the motor patterns rehearsed in the mind are similar to the ones which are produced in actual or in physical system.

Symbolic Learning Theory is yet another theory explaining the importance of mental imagery. This theory states that Visualization develops a systematic code of movement patterns, which is a mental replica in the central nervous system. It works on the principle of Positive reinforcement. Visualization assists an athlete break cycles of poor performance by imagining good performance without it happening in the first place.

Arnold Schwarzenegger who won Mr. Olympia title seven time said, "As long as the mind can envision the fact that you can do something, you can....I visualized myself being there already – having achieved the goal already. It's mind over matter."

Scientific community has given us enough evidence to prove that Visualization is the tool for the future. Someone said that if we begin to visualize, we may begin to Materialize. If you can see yourself performing a task the way you want, you can replicate the performance in actual sense as you have already practiced the event in your mind a thousand of times.

Success happens twice – first in the mind and then in reality. When you visualize, you begin to Materialize.

Mastering the Formula

"Imagination is everything. It is the preview of life's coming attractions."

Albert Einstein

The story of the Air Force Colonel George Hall, a prisoner of war in North Vietnam, during the Vietnam War, gives us the perfect example of Visualization. He was a prisoner of war and while in solitary confinement would visualize himself playing golf each day for five and a half years. With his pajamas and bare feet, lonely in his cell, he would put a golf ball down and hit his drive perfectly in imagination. He used to visualize every course that he had played on with precision and made his shots just perfect.

All the time spent as a prisoner of war finally paid off when he was released and he came back to the golf Course in the New Orleans Open, partnering with Orville Mody. During that Tournament he surprised people by hitting a 76 !

It was the best round of shot he had ever played and when a reporter congratulated him and said, "That was really what you call beginner's re-entry luck, right?" Colonel Hall smiled and said, "Not really. I never three-putted a green in all my five and a half years."

It was the visualization principles that made him perform at such a great level. In our lives, we are so busy in handling situations as they come that we forget to make use of the unlimited resource of potential which is available to us through various means. Which of the two options you would like to choose when you know you are going for an interview which means a lot to you? You may either go without preparation, or you may prepare in advance for the interview so that you are ready of every question that comes your way. Each one of us will choose the second option, because he wants to make sure the interview is just perfect. Visualization also works on the same lines, as it becomes a tool for you to prepare for any situation beforehand.

"Prepare yourself before a game by visualizing the game. See yourself facing the bowlers. Visualize the strokes you will play if he bowls in a certain manner." Sachin Tendulkar said to young players at Chinaswammy Stadium, National Cricket Academy when asked to have an interaction with young cricket players.

Have you ever thought why Rahul Dravid shadow practices shots at both ends of the pitch when we goes to bat, or why Mathew Hayden sits on the pitch on the eve of the match. These master players visualize their play in their mind. They play the match twice – once in their mind and other on the ground and that becomes a reason for their success.

ARNOLD SCHWARZENEGGER-on his success as a World Class Body Builder

The world class body builder, successful Hollywood actor, model and politician, Arnold knows the secret which makes him different from others. He knows the fact that once he has his thought focused on his Success, it becomes very easy to get on the road that leads to the Destination. Arnold uses visualization so that he sees himself through the goal he has set and this visualization then begins to transform into action through his body. His body begins to act the way he thinks, it happens because the physiology is dependent on our thoughts for directions. He says, "My mind was always in touch with my body; I felt my muscles continuously; I always took an inventory before working out. That not only helped me train; it was like meditating. I locked my mind into my muscle during training, as if I'd transplanted my mind into the tissue itself. By just thinking about it, I could actually send blood into a muscle."

Why people are called Visionaries is because they have access to their unlimited potential – the potential in the form of Imagination.

Visualize Materialize Mesmerize

"What power this is I cannot say. All that I know is that it exists."

Alexander Graham Bell

1.CHOOSE: Identify the experience where you wish to see yourself performing at extra ordinary levels. For example if you are going for an interview, then your experience will be performing well in the interview. You would like to be in a state where you are confident, speaking with energy yet being calm, giving the right answers at the right time, getting a positive response and body language from the panelist throughout your interview. In all, you have defined for yourself the experience you wish to have in reality. The first step towards achieving peak performance is to visualize yourself doing it in your mind. Let us take another example, where you wish to get a girl fall in love with you; that means that you will have to be in that perfect state in which she will fall for you. What is that state for you – is it having a lovely tonality in voice or having a pleasant personality or being caring for her or sounding impressive yet pleasing or grabbing her attention with impressive conversation. All these states are what you desire for when you meet her. Hence, the first step for you is to choose the experience where you would like to see yourself performing exceptionally.

2. EXPERIENCE: We receive inputs from our surroundings through three senses. These are Visual, Auditory and Kinesthetic. Our mind forms a model of our external environment, when it receives inputs from three

primary sources – by what we see, hear and feel. Every event of our life is been stored in our mental library with the help of these three sources of information by forming a model of the external environment which will serve as a reference for further similar kinds of experiences. For example, your performance in a presentation will be significantly affected by your performances in the previous experiences you had while giving a presentation. That is the way we think and perform. We meet a person for the first time and instantly we begin to form a model of his/her personality according to what we see, hear and feel with that person – that is the way our mind works. It looks for a pattern to match. First it will search the mind if what he sees, hears and feels can be fitted to an existing pattern in the mind, and if it is not it will begin to create a new model.

Our mind doesn't have the ability to differentiate between real and imaginary and we can take the benefit of the biological flaw of our mind's inability to differentiate and trick it into believing what we want it to through visualization thereby creating a new model or belief or reality.

After choosing the experience, your task is to form a new model which will help you perform at an altogether new level. This will be done again by providing input to your mind through three sources – Visual, Auditory and Kinesthetic, but this time the three sources are *imaginary*. Remember our mind doesn't have the ability to differentiate between reality and imagination. This new model will overwrite the previous model which existed and hence a new model will be developed. Using this model as a reference for yourself you will be able to perform at a newer level.

Creating the experience in your mind will require you to make use of your Imagination or Visualization capability. Answer few simple questions in your mind:

A. How would you like to see the experience happening in reality? Make a Picture in your mind – the place, people, actions you will be engaged into.

B. What would you like to hear when you are in that experience? Hear the sounds, noises, cheering, music etc.

C.What will you feel inside your body while experiencing the event? Feel the emotion moving in your body.

We took an example in the first step where a boy wants to develop the right states to sound impressive so that the girl may fall in love with him. In step two he will make a mental picture of which place will he meet, he sees his dressing, how he will sit – the body language he desires to have, he hears himself speaking elegantly with a soft tonality, talking total sense, visualizing the responses of the girl from time to time and seeing her getting in awe of the conversation. Both feeling care for each other and developing an interest. It is like mentally rehearsing the event, before getting in there.

Doing such an exercise, he mentally rehearses the full event and it becomes very easy for him to go out there and replicate the states which he experienced in his mind. Remember irrespective of where you have practiced the event, you become an expert at it with repetition, because your mind doesn't have the ability to differentiate between the real and the imaginary.

3. GO LIVE: The third and the final step in achieving peak performance is to go there in the field and act. You have had a mental rehearsal of your future, which has given you a practice of the reality – your motor skills, your thoughts, your emotions and feelings are right there with you to deliver the results you achieved in your mind successfully. It is just like making a cake after you know all the ingredients and the process of how they inter relate among each other and give you the final output.

The secret to extra-ordinary living is to trick your mind into forming new success patterns which over ride the pre-existing diseased patterns.

The Key to Visualization
lies here

"Imagination is the beginning of creation. You imagine what you desire; you will what you imagine; and at last you create what you will."

George Bernard Shaw

To get maximum results of Visualization, the focus should be on few simple principles which enhance the experiences of the exercise.

1. Repetition: The frequency of the Visualization has a big effect on performance, because it is just like developing a muscle. The more you work out, the bigger and better results you are going to get. Hammering your mind with the same images, voices, and emotion will create positive lasting impression on your beliefs and mind models. Breaking away your old negative models of mind and forging new successful empowering beliefs.

2. Intensity: The intensity with which sunlight falls on earth directly affects the Earth's temperature. And intensity of your thoughts has direct effect on the results you will get in achieving a state of Peak Performance. When you visualize, make the picture in your mind brighter, sharper and rather than seeing a picture in your mind, see yourself in a three-dimensional movie, where you see yourself reaching a particular experience which you desire very easily. Make the picture large in size and make it come closer to you in your mind. Your intensity will vary according to whether you are in an associated state or a dissociated state. Associated state means when you

don't see your face in the mental picture because you are in the first position, you see your hands, legs and the surrounding because you are inside the body. Whereas a dissociated state would be when in the mental picture you are observing your body from outside – seeing your face, hands, back, legs and how you performing in the picture from outside. Being in an associated state is more powerful and generates intense emotion while visualizing the experience and much more productive during the process.

3. Time: The time of the Visualizations affects your body state in a big way. When you have just finished off with the Visualization exercise you will be in a peak state of that experience for some time till other thoughts start setting in your mind. So if you need to deliver at some particular time, do a visualization exercise just before such a time to get instant results. Cricketers understand that timing is so very significant in delivering performance. When they get on to the pitch they will play some random shots on the pitch just before they face the delivery. They visualize how they will play in reality just before the game starts. It is not because they have not practiced the whole season but because they are setting themselves in the game before the actual game starts.

Our mind has a powerful capacity to replicate performances – Visualize your Best Performance first and then let it guide you in Reality

It's not hocus pocus it's about Focus

"All that we are is the result of what we have thought."

Buddha

We feel emotionally low because we see ourselves feeling low in our minds. Don't you remember a time when you were extremely happy and suddenly on a thought of a negative experience you begin to feel the change . You begin to focus on that negative thought and on a moment's notice you change your happiness to grief. Challenge is how to get rid of the negative aura as quickly as possible. The solution lies in shifting our focus from negative to positive, from dis-empowering thought to an empowering one, from a useless state to a useful state.

A very popular exercise many Motivational Gurus practice in their session is focused on Visualization, here it goes:

Close your eyes, go into your mind and imagine yourself stepping out of your body. You observe yourself standing on the stage and a spot light over you. You have a complete 360 degree view of yourself standing. Ignore all your flaws and weaknesses which you possess. Make your picture as bright as possible; you look like a big person standing on the center stage without any flaws. Put a background music which motivates you – it can be any music which makes you feel good. See yourself from every direction. See the positive traits of your personality in your body. Enhance your experience by seeing your body performing at its best with the positive personality traits it possesses. Imagine as if the body is replete with confidence, energy, self esteem and power. It has all the qualities you would desire it to have. Now step into your body and feel all the qualities flowing within you. You feel being energized by the qualities of your body and now you are in the spot light on the center stage of your mind. You are all powerful as you thought and in a new state.

Use this exercise to enhance your positive side of your personality or when you need to make use of the best in yourself.

It makes one feel better when there is a shift of focus from the negative to the positive, the choice of which lies with us.

Learn Unlearn and Relearn

Ever noticed why only few people become successful in this world, why twenty percent of the people own eighty percent of the wealth, why only few among zillions get an opportunity to live their life of dreams. There is nothing special in it, even you can achieve what people like Richard Branson, Robin Sharma, Britney Spears or The Beatles have achieved, only if you get to know their formula of making things happen in their lives. Using their beliefs and value system which helped them in achieving a specific outcome in their field, you could get similar outcomes in your field. It is like going on a mountaineering expedition to the world's highest peak, following the path laid down by others who have successfully reached the top. You may encounter several paths, but once you have found out the most effective path it is only a matter of action and in no time powerful results will begin to surface.

Success leaves Clues!

"Many of us spend our lives searching for success when it is usually so close that we can reach out and touch it."

Russel H. Conwell

There was a baker in Africa who was widely popular for the special chocolate nut cake he used to make in his bakery. People would travel long distances just to buy cakes for themselves and their family from his shop. One day, a person named Jack, who was a baker boy in a nearby town, visited the famous baker's house and showed his interest in learning the process the baker followed. The famous baker said to him, "Anyone can make the cake I make in my bakery, if he gets my recipe". And he handed over the recipe to the boy. Since that day, his life changed because he became a millionaire few months later, by selling cakes with the new recipe he received from the Baker. It was the new found recipe which made all the difference in his life. The lesson this story gives us is that, we can replicate patterns of success in our lives by following the processes followed by successful people. These successful people are experienced enough to make the best success cakes and to make the same success cake means to replicate the model of success they followed.

Let us take the example of KFC – Kentucky Fried Chicken, which is a chain of fast food restaurants selling the famous fried chicken. It was the recipe of Colonel Harland Sanders which made it into such a big brand all over the World. He had the famous recipe of making finger licking tasty fried chicken. Now when KFC has expanded they use the same recipe at all their outlets and hence the chicken they serve is similar in taste and aroma all across. Sitting in Canada, one can have the taste of the chicken similar to that made by Colonel Harland Sanders sitting in the US. How is it possible? It has become possible because they used the same process and the same set of ingredients all across their outlets. That is what I call as replicating the recipe and getting the similar results.

We have always said that Success leaves clues. What are the clues left by some of the Leaders we admire? Mother Teresa left the clue of Compassion, Abraham Lincoln left it in the form of Persistence, Steve Jobs who is the co-founder of Apple leaves it in the form of Innovation, and Mahatma Gandhi left it in form of Giving. These clues are the qualities which these successful people acquired in course of their journey. Even today, we admire them for these qualities and take examples from their lives.

They developed these qualities because they had developed unique distinctions in how, why and what they think in their minds which made them different from others. What happened in their minds was of more interest to us because they used certain mental processes which were highly effective and useful. How good would it be if we were to have access to the processes they used in their mind to master a skill, quality or talent. Such a formula would be more than just a process; it might be something which can help us transform the way we get results, the way we perform a certain skill or the way we develop a talent for something which is beneficial to us. Imagine having compassion like Mandela, persistence like Lance Armstrong, skill like Ronaldo, talent like Don

Bradman etc. Such qualities if acquired can certainly give us amazing results in our lives.

If we see it from a different perspective, these people who have mastered a skill or a quality or a talent, are the same bakers who have an excellent recipe for making the famous chocolate nut cake. People love to come to their bakery to eat those cakes and take examples of their cake's preparation where ever they go. And you and I are the baker boy of a nearby town, who desire to change our lives by learning to make the cake which gives us prosperity and abundance. The bigger question is – Can we replicate the success recipe and become successful ourselves by learning from others. The answer is Yes, when we wish to learn a new skill or acquire a talent or wish to get the results some other person has got, we can replicate and deliver. But How?

Any kind of Success can be replicated once we get to know the Strategy that is being used to get a desired outcome.

Unraveling secrets of "Successful" beings

"Anyone who stops learning is old, whether at twenty or eighty. Anyone who keeps earning stays young. The greatest thing in life is to keep your mind young."

Henry Ford

Step 1: CHOOSE: Choose a skill or a talent you would like to acquire. For example, you might wish to develop public speaking ability, so the first step you will take is to choose it as a skill which you like to master. Our aim is to find where we are and where we want to go and then fill in the gap with the right talent and skills. Sometimes we are too afraid of ourselves because we are not adept in facing our fears. If a salesperson is not happy with the results he is getting as compared with his peers he has two choices – either he stays the same or he finds out what is stopping him from achieving those desired results. Is it communication or body language or what not? But the first task he has to engage in is finding out the big Why of his failure. Success is more about finding out the why, and less about finding the how. Once the why is clear the how will automatically surface. Now that he is clear whether it is his communication or the way he prospects a customer, he knows what will bridge the gap between his present and future performance. That is the first step to attain the desired success in our outcomes.

Find the area of your life which if you develop will assist you in whatever activity you are engaged in i.e. your job, work, study, play etc.

Step 2: IDENTIFY: I would ask you to identify three people who have done excellently well in the area which you wish to improve in. They should be the ones who are successful, the ones whom you admire, who have made a difference in their fields with their Performance.

For example, if someone needs to develop presentation skills, one needs to find out people who have made it big using their presentation skills and so the three people who may act as a reference point may be leaders like Zig Ziglar, Barack Obama and Abrahm Lincoln. Or if you want to develop a habit of perseverance identify people who are pioneers in perseverance like Lance Armstrong, Michael Jordan and Oprah Winfrey. It is just like a process of finding the baker who makes the best cake in the World, who has the best recipe.

Identify the three people whom you like to model, they can even be any one from your friends, family, peers, co-workers, boss or any celebrity, it can just be anyone whom you admire because of the skill they possess. You may choose – a parent, a musician, an entertainer, an athlete, a friend or a relative. Throughout your life, you would have definitely found out that there are at least three people to whom, you look up to, and those you can call your role models in the field you like to get quality results in.

Step 3: ANSWER: Ask questions to yourself which give you an insight on how the people you have chosen made a quality difference in their lives by using that skill. Questions assist you in knowing the success patterns they followed, the methods they used, the pre requisite skills they had, their thinking patterns, their psychology, the tools they used and many more. It is a process to know the recipe of the best cake. It is to know where to start and what to finish.

Question 1: What does the person do, that is different from other people?

This question gives you the answer to the activities, tools they used that made them hugely successful and that what differentiates them from the others. Let us take the example of a man who has been a pioneer in innovation and a person who lived for self improvement – Benjamin Franklin. Anyone who wishes to model Benjamin would like to model his Value System. He chose thirteen value parameters to evaluate himself on a daily basis and on his evaluation he used to score points across each value he had listed in his diary. This helped him make better choices according to his value system, which gave him enough self control and wisdom he required for success. This is what made him into what he was – an innovator, a scientist, an inventor, a statesman, a printer, a philosopher, a musician, and an economist. That is such a big thought for us, that to manage and follow our values, we may make tremendous difference in the choices we make daily.

One of the concepts in human psychology is Observational learning. It is a process of learning the behavioral patterns and new information by observing the behaviors of others. Imagine you wish to become a stage artist, and so you will observe experienced and successful stage artists performing at an event. And this way you will gain insights into the behavior and attitudes such people carry to become successful. These behavioral insights and information would become powerful tools for you to carry out a performance though not similar but close to the original levels of performance of the artists.

Now let us say that you wish to model Jordan, what should you do to find out the difference point when you compare him with others? You will see his videos – how he dunks the ball, when he takes the jump; his body language – what moves he makes, how he walks on the floor; the training – is there any special kind of training he takes, what sports gear he uses, what is his diet etc. All these things are nothing more than tools and answers to the most powerful question "What should I do on a daily basis to become who I want to become". Answer is to model people who have been there, done that. Be selective; find out things which make people successful in your area of interest and which you can follow to get the same results that other people achieved.

Question 2: What does your role model do which you don't do in your life?

All the successful people give us strategies to succeed, and there is no need to try out different strategies by ourselves and learn the same thing. When you want to get the results faster, find out what works and what doesn't. There is absolutely no need to spend time on activities which don't produce desirable result. There is a saying – "We are never going to live long enough to commit all the mistakes of the World". This makes us realize the need to learn things from people who have already tried various approaches and have become pioneers in their respective fields.

But where do we get to know which strategy works and which doesn't? Find out what tools and training did your role model use to get to where he is right now. What do they say to themselves when they are involved in their jobs, what is their mental state – are they excited, passionate, calm, aggressive, compassionate etc. When you see that the results you are getting are not reaping the right results, why stick to the same strategies or thinking and remain at the same level. Why do the same things and expect different results, rather do things differently to get different results. Find the approach which gives you result and simply move ahead to learn something new. How come you see so many billionaires in the age group of 20s? It is just because of the basic reason that they have learnt to learn from mistakes of the successful and model their strategies to become successful.

Question 3: What are the behavioral patterns of that person?

Michael Jordan is known for his never give up attitude. He said in a commercial about the ability he developed in himself to conquer failures – the never giving up attitude.

"I've missed more than 9000 shots in my career. I've lost almost 300 games. Twenty-six times I've been trusted to take the game winning shot and missed. I've failed over and over and over again in my life. And that is why I succeed." – Michael Jordan

Why not replicate that ability and have it in our own lives. Now when you face a failure why not remember the behavioral pattern of your role model Jordan and show the same never give up attitude.

If you are into communication, why not have a look at the way Oprah Winfrey talks. Apart from her excellent communication, what makes her different is that she appears to have a genuine interest in people and an ability to make a deep emotional connection with them at all levels. That's what differentiates an Oprah Winfrey from other television hosts. Understanding their behavior makes modeling a lot easier to implement and get better desirable results.

But there is a difference between "learning" and "performing" the behavior. The behavior learnt may not be the one which is performed. But our aim should be to reduce the difference between what is acquired or learnt and what is performed. This depends on two basic factors:

1. Retention: Are you able to retain all of their behavior or only in parts. Sometimes people tend to miss out a lot of information and strategies being used by their role model while they acquire information. Hence the ability to retain what is learnt makes a lot of difference in deliverance.

2. Replication: Sometimes it becomes a powerful learning experience once you get to know what kind of skill is to be acquired for modeling certain actions of your role model and that becomes your key. Now if one day you observe a rope walker and as soon as you reach home, you begin to model him, it would be altogether different. Because in performing the act, the rope walker had acquired several skills prior to his action. And if you learn what skills are required for getting to that level you have done your job successfully. Once you know the skills required, you get to the next level and begin modeling his actions and behavior which will give you the results you are looking for.

WHAT SKILL OR CAPACITIES DOES YOUR ROLE MODEL HAVE?
CAPACITIES AND SKILLS

WHY DOES YOUR ROLE MODEL HAVE THAT SKILL?
PRINCIPLES AND BELIEFS

HOW DOES YOUR ROLE MODEL HAVE IT?
ACTIONS, THINKING STRATEGIES AND FOCUS

SUCCESS MODEL CHART

What to Model Capacities and skills	**Self or You** What are your skills? Where are you standing Now?	**Role Model** For what skills do you approve of your role model? Why is he so special?	**Difference** Which skills does your role model have that you don't have?
Behavior with self/others/at Work/during Performance	What behavior you desire to change in self? What kind of attitude is dis-empowering you?	What is the disposition of your role model? How does he think - define his mental conditioning.	What separates your behavior from the behavior you wish to model? Where lies the difference?
Value system, Beliefs	What defines your priorities? What are care values which determine your actions?	Define the value system of your role model? Why he acts the way he acts? What beliefs does your role model have about himself? What is the underlying purpose for doing the activity?	Is there a difference between the two value system? Is it possible to have congruence?
Actions, Strategies, Focus	What actions do you take on a daily basis to get the outcome you desire?	Why does he get different and more powerful results? Does he follow a different set of action to get to the outcome?	What are you not doing which is costing so much of energy without results? List down the actions that you are NOT taking to get the results you desire.

Start Sound Action

"Get action. Seize the moment. Man was never intended to become an oyster."

Theodore Roosevelt

Taking action is primal for any change to take place in your life. Very famous quote says "Logic will not change an emotion, only motion can change an emotion". No amount of thinking is equal to the little action you take for yourself. People are great thinkers but Leaders are great implementers. Now that you have an inventory of the strategies, tools, best practices and empowering behavioral patterns, next step is to start implementing those strategies in your daily lives and see yourself getting the results you desire at a much faster pace. Let us say you wish to know what needs to be done on a daily basis to make your life significant – take the example of Steve Jobs, who on a daily basis answers a question to make his life priorities clear "*If today were the last day of my life, would I want to do what I am about to do today?*" Would this question serve as an excellent guide for you to do the things which really matter?

Tools for success are almost everywhere, find them, select them, use them and reuse them, that's what will make your journey a beautiful one.

Once you become aware of a successful model, go in the real world and begin testing your model. Is this giving you the result you desire? If a model works for someone doesn't necessarily mean it will work for you, because every human is different, you will never find another you. Sometimes model begin to give results when they are customized. Try to change the model according to your needs and requirements – customize the model you have learnt, take out a few things and add something from your side. This is a process of refining the model which goes on until the time you start getting results – make as many changes as possible to get the same or even better result than your role model. Testing brings measurable results on the surface. Once you have found the model which gives you success patterns as you desire – cement the model in your behavior.

Act on the "Success Model Chart" to know the strategies, skills and processes which can make a complete shift in the way you get results – this would be your Roadmap.

The Thrilling Formula – Imagine and Act

"Charge your future! As you recreate this positive force in your life, take big, massive leaps into your future. Be imaginative, bold and brave! The results may surprise you."

Jim Allen

Learning modeling is a fun way to use your potential to get results, and an excellent way to fasten the self learning process. Daily challenges will demand us to not only use observational learning as a tool for daily successful achievements of Goals, but also to make moment by moment choices on life's matter. Every moment of our lives we are making choices, even when you pick this book you have made a choice, when you choose the direction of your career you make a choice, when you engage in any activity you make a choice, saying a yes or a no is again a matter of choice.

The greatest challenge of life is to make decisions every day, every hour, every second and every moment. You may lose a lot in life by making wrong choices and then repent on the choice you made at the first place. Remember the last time you made a choice which cost you hell lot of stress. That is okay if you make a couple of bad choices, and it serves as a good learning lesson. But here we are talking about achieving peak performances, which is more than just learning, it is less of failures and more of success, lack of stress and abundance of results, fewer do-ables and significant deliverables.

Let us assume you have to make a difficult choice right now and see how your mind works. Your mind will evaluate the situation, look at the past models of an event of the same nature or something which is close to the scenario at hand – it will evaluate the options on your core belief patterns and make a choice dependent on your past choices on that matter – rarely does it oppose the existing mental models. That is how thinking takes place in our mind. If we follow the same thinking pattern we are going to get the same outcomes in our lives. To change the outcomes you have to change the way you make choices.

We are going to learn an advanced stage of "Role Modeling", which we discussed in the last chapter. This would enhance our capacity to make choices on the most basic level. Suppose the most basic level of an object is atom, similarly the most basic level of decision making is every moment or instant. Role Modeling is all about choosing the most harmonious path to achieve your outcomes while the advanced stage is about sustaining yourself on the track you have chosen for yourself. The directional conditioning takes place in Role Modeling, but your mental conditioning occurs in the advance stage.

The outcomes you have received in your life were a result of your past or existing thought patterns or your beliefs. To forge a future of your choice which goes beyond the ordinary you need to follow a altogether different pattern, which serves as a reference point, guide or a compass for your decision making. When you model a person's thought pattern and belief systems you begin to get the same results that the person achieved. The reason why I say this is because your focus doesn't remain only on the actions and skills which are external influencers but you also put your focus on internal mental processes i.e. the thoughts and beliefs of the Model you choose for yourself.

Step 1: IDENTIFY: The person who has the behavior you want for yourself. For example, let us say I am stuck in a situation where I need to show temperance. I will choose Mahatma Gandhi, because he is an epitome for me when I consider temperance.

Step 2: FOCUS: On how the person looks, see his facial features, hear his voice inside your mind, look at the way he talks, how he speaks, what is his body language, how will he say and what will he say and feel the emotion your model will feel once he is in a similar situation you are in. Aim is to make a clear mental picture of your role model in your mind.

Step 3: IMAGINE: Close your eyes and imagine yourself stepping into the body of your role model – seeing through his eyes, people looking at you with the same grace, charm, and excitement as if every word you speak is the word spoken by your role model, you acquire his skills, talents and behavior. After you imagine yourself in that stage, take your imagination to the present situation or challenge you are facing in decision making. Now see yourself with new attitude, behavior and thought pattern acquired from your role model and look at the challenge with his eyes. Note that you have surrendered your thinking to your role model. And then answer these questions:

1. *What will I do, if it were my role model inside me*
2. *How will I do, if it were my role model inside me*
3. *What will I say, if it were my role model inside me*

4. *How will I say, if it were my role model inside me*

5. *What will I like to see, if it were my role model inside me*

6. *What will I choose, if it were my role model inside me*

Step 4: ACT: Act your choices with conviction and commitment and see yourself getting amazing unbelievable results. In the previous step you got to know the best choice out of all the choices available and besides it you have also evaluated those choices with a reference point i.e. having your role model's though pattern.

Viewing a challenge with someone else's eyes will not only give you the best solutions but also give you a third person point of view which is completely new to us.

Director to an Actor – "You better get into the Character"

"I think, therefore I am."

Descartes

Let us imagine an evening, when you are completely tired with all your work that you have been doing since morning, the bout of fight you had with your spouse, children giving you a tough time, pestering you for hours. Suddenly, your cell phone rings and you get to know that your old friend is waiting downstairs and he wants to meet you. What do you do! You immediately rush to the washroom, clean your face, comb your hair and wear some beautiful clothes, stand in front of your mirror and give a big smile and start acting *as if* you are perfectly fine. You go down and meet your friend behaving *as if* you are not tired, having a cup of coffee you begin to talk normally *as if* you were stress free, when he asks you about your family life, you act *as if* it is in a perfect state. We have been an expert in behaving *as if* something has happened or not, *as if* we feel an emotion or not, *as if* we love someone or not, and this has been one of the greatest revolutions in human performances.

Let us say you had a bad day at home, when you left for office your car's tyre punctures, you see a huge traffic jam ahead of you, you are getting calls from office asking you about the status of yesterday's work, and you have a very important client meeting scheduled in afternoon. You finally reach for the meeting on time. Would you like to showcase the troubles you had experienced since morning when you left for office to the client? The answer is no, so what will you do is that you will act *as if* you had the best day ever, you behave *as if* the sunshine was amazing, *as if* there was no traffic on roads, *as if* you had a comfortable journey throughout. You act *as if* you are completely confident, *as if* you are the best man to deal with, *as if* you have a good control on your life. When you behave *as if* everything was beautiful, you start to pass on this feeling to your client and he sees confidence in your words. Ultimately, you win and you succeed in getting past the offer, because you acted *as if* you are going to be successful.

Everyone on this planet has some or the other challenge, difficulty or fear to face. We are somehow in total capacity to live beyond these difficulties and fears and make our lives better. Most people get into the mode of this negative thinking and begin to believe that these challenges and difficulties control their behavior, actions and emotions and hence they behave negatively. It is only because they are disturbed internally that they create disturbances for others. So the question comes how to change ourselves internally, so that we are not controlled by the shackles of our negative circumstances. One of the powerful ways to do that is to use a phenomenon which we use in our daily lives – act *as if*. As soon as the negative emotion begins to affect you, act *as if* you are in control, *as if* you have the power to resolve internal conflicts, *as if* your positive energy is working for you, *as if* you are confident, *as if* everything around is working the way you desired. When you begin to act *as if*, there is a shift in your mental process which is focused on the negative and it shows you a new direction altogether – a positive one, i.e. which will empower you to see things with an optimistic lens.

> *Whether you act as if you are confident or a failure, in both the cases you become what you think about.*

The two way Winning Link: Action and Feeling

"All that you accomplish or fail to accomplish with your life is the direct result of your thoughts."

James Allen

The psychologists have done enough research on how our thoughts control our actions, but little are they aware that our actions also control our thoughts. Our psychological processes cause our behaviors and actions, which means that we act in a particular way because we are thinking particular thoughts, or experiencing a particular emotion. Scientists now believe that the reverse is also true. If we commit to a particular action or emotion, our physiology tends to generate corresponding thoughts, images, and energy vibrations in our body. In Unlimited Power, Tony Robbins says, "If you change your physiology – that is, your posture, breathing patterns, muscle tension, facial expressions, gestures, movements, words, vocal tonality – you instantly change your internal representations and your state."

Let us do a small exercise – say this statement aloud "I feel energetic", with your hands hanging beside your waist, shoulders drooping forward. Gauge the level of energy you posses after you say this statement. Now again repeat the same statement again, but this time you need to straighten your shoulders and clap your hands vigorously while you make this statement. Now again feel the energy levels in your body. You will find on experiencing these two states that your energy levels shot by almost five hundred percent when you clapped your hands with your shoulders straight. Do you remember the time when this statement was shouted at you at least hundreds of time by your school teacher "You crazy chap – better Sit up Straight or I will..." Because the teacher knew that she will get you into an attentive state by changing your body posture.

Psychological evidence proves that certain body positions cause certain types of emotions in our body. In a study, researchers found that people who sit up straight were more likely to believe thoughts they wrote down, while in that posture, concerning whether they were qualified for a job or not. And the ones who slumped on their chair were less likely to accept the feelings which were written down, about their ability. This study showed how their body postures had an effect on their feelings.

Let us take an example of the time we are happy. We are happy and hence we smile, but the reverse is also, when we smile we become happy too. In a class, when you are not able to concentrate what is the first thing you do? You straighten your back, pull back your shoulders, open your eyes wide, and tighten your facial muscles – you change your body language to change your internal state. Even in yoga, postures play an important part because they change how you feel inside your body. Have not you heard that yoga postures assist people to develop emotions like happiness, confidence, energy etc inside one's body? All these examples illustrate a simple point that there is a deep connection between our external actions or body language and our internal emotions.

We can take benefit from such a discovery by behaving and acting corresponding to the feeling we require to instill in our body. Once the body begins to acquire such a feeling then our mind can make all the necessary biological changes to reach to that desired state. For example let us say you wish to feel more confident right now, what will you do? Act as if you are extremely confident, have the body language of a confident person you know, talk as if you are confident about whatever you are saying, dress yourself as if confidence is what comes from you and I can promise you that confidence will begin to develop inside your body. Your mind will make all the chemical changes to make your feel more confident.

There is something very interesting about the way we dress and the effect our dressing has on our attitudes. You can make out the difference in the way you talk, walk, and present yourself to others when you are wearing a formal suite verses wearing your shorts. The difference in attitude is not due to the change in internal thinking but a change in your external being, which initiated a change in your internal thinking.

The "father of psychology" William James who was the founder of the American Society for Psychical Research said, "Action seems to follow feeling, but really action and feeling go together; and by regulating the action, which is under the more direct control of the will, we can indirectly regulate the feeling, which is not."

There is an intimate relation between mind and body, which is two way – mind affecting your actions and your actions affecting your mind, somehow we forget to use the latter link.

You Become Your Beliefs

Did you challenge your beliefs today? Did you ever de-condition yourself in the past? Have you ever re-written your beliefs? If the answer to any one of the question is "no", it means you have missed a great deal of your potential. You become your beliefs, and if these beliefs are not conditioned for success, it ecomes utterly challenging to give your best. Have you not seen ew people who are always replete with energy and passion owards what they are doing! Don't be surprised but they are the nes who have conditioned themselves for success. Their work ecomes play and they are enjoying and dancing every moment. ligning your beliefs to success is like correcting your compass hich guides you to your destination. Once the compass begins to ork, showing the right direction, it becomes easy for you to guide ourself towards the ultimate destination – the pinnacle of success.

The science of achieving your Potential

"Man often becomes what he believes himself to be. If I keep on saying to myself that I cannot do a certain thing, it is possible that I may end by really becoming incapable of doing it. On the contrary, if I have the belief that I can do it, I shall surely acquire the capacity to do it even if I may not have it at the beginning."

Mahatma Gandhi

Challenge a man's belief and this is what he will say, "Do you mean to say I am mad, don't you tell me you mad guy! This is what I believe in, how dare you challenge me". This is the sanctity our beliefs hold for ourselves, almost like a religion. This is what is been addressed in this chapter – your Belief is your religion.

The greatest question that has intrigued the human race is – how does our mind make decisions and choices? After several experiment and studies it was found out that our mind thinks in only patterns an models. These patterns have their origin in the belief system. Belief i anything that we hold or assume to be true. They are assumed truths tha are embedded in our subconscious mind and cause our behavior an action on a day to day basis.

Until we are presented with some series of events that prove o beliefs wrong, we never tend to question our beliefs. Because they a habitual in nature, beliefs differentiate between people being happy a sad. A person who has happiness as the core belief when becomes sad, t sadness would be temporary, but if a sad person experiences pain, t sadness is bound to last long. The reason is based on science of our mi When you have a positive belief system, and experience joy there certain chemicals called neuropeptides, which are released and are th received by your millions of receptors of the brain. These receptors are the same ones that accept outside chemicals like heroin, alcohol and even aspirin. The more these receptors are used less effective they become and your brain then again has to produce the same neuropeptides to feed new receptors and hence you remain positive almost all the time, as your brain is consistently producing the joy chemical needed to satiate the receptors. Now if you feel a negative thought the neuropeptides which are related to negative thought are produced, but your receptors are habitual to the joy chemical so they will again ask the brain to produce those positive chemicals and hence you don't remain sad for a long time. But if a person has a negative belief system, his mind produces neuropeptides of that emotions and it will produce more of it to feed the receptors because they demand more of that chemical, so it's a chain reaction to happiness or sadness. So this puts us back on the driver's seat of our lives.

Only your Belief System has access to the reservoirs of unlimited potential available to you.

Two sides of the Coin: Placebo and Nocebo

"A belief is not merely an idea the mind possesses; it is an idea that possesses the mind."

Robert Oxton Bolt

Many a times doctors give a fake medicine which is called Placebo, a medicine which has no curative agent and is nothing but a sugar pill or a saline solution. The patients are made to believe that they have been given a medication which is bound to cure their disease. And what they have observed after administering the placebo to the diseased patient is miraculous. They found that the body responded to the placebos by having the same effect which a pure medicine was to induce. The question then comes – does our belief system has an effect on healing of the body. What is important here is that the patients were made to believe that something is done. The placebo was supplemented by a belief that the medicine has the curative power to better the health of the person. With their belief, their body started to respond in the same way as if the actual medicine has been administered, producing the same chemical reactions which are meant to cure the problem they are facing. This experiment goes on to prove a fact that the power of belief is far beyond what we have thought about belief.

Having talked about healing through belief which is called the placebo effect, its counterpart is called the Nocebo effect. Nocebo effect means that if you have a belief that something will harm you, even though it is harmless, will start harming you. There was a case of a man, who in a fit of rage over a fight with his family members took around twenty sleeping pills at one time. Realizing that he had done a grave mistake, he asked his neighbor to take him to the hospital because he thought he had taken a huge overdose and he started to feel unconscious. When he reached the hospital, it was found that his blood pressure was seemingly low and he was breathing rapidly. He was tested and given the treatment, and was then told by the doctor that the medicines he had taken were completely harmless. On knowing this his blood pressure immediately came to normal and breathing restored to normal pace.

Bruce Lipton, a cellular biologist said, "I was exhilarated by the new realization that I could change the character of my life by changing my beliefs. I was instantly energized because I realized that there was a science – based path that would take me from my job as a perennial "victim" to my new position as "co-creator" of my destiny (Prologue, xv)". It gives us enough evidence that our beliefs drive our outcomes and especially our thinking reflects the quality of life we are going to Live. Negative thinking evolves negative outcomes both at physical and internal levels.

Become the master of your Destiny by transforming the quality of your Beliefs – the placebo and the nocebo effect are working 24 hrs a day.

Did you Question your Beliefs today!

"To believe in the things you can see and touch is no belief at all. But to believe in the unseen is both a triumph and a blessing."

Bob Proctor

The child is always perfect in his thinking until he gets educated by the real world of illusionary boundaries and limits, which he has been taught not to question. We were taught that a man could not fly and soon Wright brothers made it possible; we were taught our World is flat, yet there were certain people questioned the belief and proved that Earth is round; we were taught that a man could not make a difference in lives of billions by helping the poor and the sick, yet one lady broke the beliefs and spread her message across the Globe – she was Mother Teresa; we believed humans cannot carry their phones with them, yet today each one of us is having a personal cell phone; we were taught that to become a billionaire, one must get education, yet we see, read and know people who beyond their odds became insanely rich and successful; we were told that we couldn't go to moon, yet many countries have already flagged the moon.

But a true example of a belief barrier being broken by human race occurred in 1954. For thousands of years it was thought that no one can run a mile within 4 minutes. It was believed that human performance would not allow us to break the four minute mile barrier. Yet, in 1954, one man named Roger Bannister broke this performance barrier by running one mile in little less than four minutes. He achieved this impossible task not merely by the physical training that he had undergone, but by consistently questioning his existing belief that no one can run a one mile distance within four minutes. He instilled a belief in his mind that he will run the distance within four minutes thereby giving his body a command to deliver results he desired instead of delivering the results in accordance of the limits put by others. And it was not the performance barrier which was tested and broken but the dis-empowering belief barrier.

As per our conditioning, we are made to believe that there are certain possibilities and impossibilities. Time and again individuals from our neighborhood have gone and proved that impossibilities are in our minds and not in the physical world. When we start questioning our beliefs we begin the process of self transformation, we get rid of our old belief models and evolve ourselves with new powerful high performance models. Next time you come across a situation when you are told this seems impossible challenge your mind to go beyond what is said. Create doubt on your beliefs in your mind by remembering the time it had happened or if it has not happened in reality, use the visualization tool and make it happen in your mind. Remember when you visualize you materialize. Questioning our limiting beliefs is the first step to peak performance.

Have you not seen in a circus where the big elephant will be tied up with a thin rope while a small elephant tied with a big strong rope? It has nothing to do with the size of the elephant but the size of the beliefs. In his childhood, the elephant is tied up with a big strong rope to keep him from trying to get away. He will try hard to get rid of the chains, but will not be able to succeed in his mission. Now this elephant which has grown into a big mammoth, believes that he could not break free from the rope even if he tried to, because his belief has conditioned him to think that it is impossible to break the rope, and so is tied with a thin rope. In our lives too, we have been chained by our fears which in actual are fragile ropes which are waiting to be broken away by our beliefs. Do the thing which stops you from performing your best – it is like running towards your fears instead of running away from them, the more you run away, the more chances that they will catch up with you. Visualize as if you don't have the fear in the first place. Recall the incidents when you were able to overcome your fear and delivered excellent results and think about them again and again. This will not only familiarize you with your true performance but help you transform your old rotten beliefs into optimistic ones.

OPRAH WINFREY-the Belief Machine

The stories of rags to riches have many names to them, which include of special girl born to an unwed mother, in a small town of Mississippi. She woke up to a challenging world only to find that she was poor, black and a female. From the age of six to thirteen prior to the time when she went to stay with her father, she was sexually abused by her mother's male relatives and another visitor, which was emotionally devastating to her. The misery didn't stop there; she was then admitted to a detention center, only to be refused admission on account of no vacancy. All these events in her life didn't shape her beliefs, because she believed in her talent of understanding and communicating with people and using it as a tool of Success. She said, "Every time you state what you want or believe, you're the first to hear it. It's a message to both you and others about what you think is possible. Don't put a ceiling on yourself." She believed in her talents to an extent that she left the school to join a local channel as an anchor and a reporter. What happened after that is history – she is known for the utterly popular self-titled talk show, which has won zillions of awards, she herself has appeared in the Forbes list of most powerful celebrity multiple times.

We are operating with habitual thinking and behavior, which keeps us at the same level as we are and doesn't let us go beyond our limitations to utilize our intellectual, mental, physical reserves. The habitual thinking in bees is very similar to what the humans have. In an experiment, a big seven gallon jar was taken and filled with bees, and was wrapped with a plastic sheet from the head. The setup was made such that there is enough air for the bees to live for forty eight hours. These bees would continuously buzz around and try to move outside the glass jar by banging on the plastic sheet. After letting the plastic sheet on for complete forty eight hours, it was removed. Ninety nine percent of the bees still remained inside because they developed wrong belief patterns about their behavior and abilities. What we as humans do is very similar. We begin to create our own patterns of belief, about our abilities, potentials, skills and talents based on our external environment, the same as bees did for themselves. We begin to judge and evaluate based on our experiences and make the beliefs very strong in a very short duration of time. Biologically humans have resisted change in any form and hence the outcome is that we never question our disabilities as we don't like change, we like to keep believing in our disabilities. And instead we are always in a process of questionings our abilities. The lesson we draw from various examples is only one that we need to question our belief system every moment and visualize the impossible, breaking through our limitations.

Believe, not in your disabilities but in your abilities,
not in your boundaries but in your potential,
not in what stops you but what liberates you.

Your Treasure lies in your Reference Points

"If you believe in what you are doing, then let nothing hold you up in your work. Much of the best work of the world has been done against seeming impossibilities. The thing is to get the work done."

Dale Carnegie

In 1954, Roger Bannister broke the four minute mile barrier, even when there had been no development in sports psychology and no new path breaking discovery in human sciences. He broke this record by merely imagining himself breaking the barrier in his mind long before he actually did it. He began the process of changing his belief even when no one had done it before. This is called instilling a belief which had never occurred in reality. The surprise in case of Roger Bannister was not his breaking the record after thousands of years, but the after effects. Within a year of his breaking the four minute mile barrier thirty seven other runners also broke it and the following year three hundred other runners also did the same even when there was no path breaking discovery in achieving peak performances. The phenomenon was possible because Roger Bannister changed the reference points of other athletes from the impossible to the possible. And surprisingly it had nothing to do with physical practice, the barrier was only mental when other runners were able to see themselves breaking the four minute mile barrier in their minds they manifested it in reality. When the seemingly impossible result was broken in physical reality it led other runners to believe that it is possible for humans to break the barrier. The most important thing to note is that other runners saw with their eyes the breaking of record by

Roger Bannister, which ultimately changed their belief. Hence for us to get extra-ordinary results there is a need to see ourselves breaking our belief barrier which exists in the mind and not in reality. Whether you see it in your mind or in reality it makes no difference as our mind does not have the ability to differentiate between the two.

It is similar to how the computer works which displays an output based on the input provided. Whether the input is provided to the computer through a keyboard or a mouse, the software processes the input according to its logic and system thereby gives an output accordingly. It does not depend on the source of input. Our mind has a similar system where our Belief System is the software been inputted by our external environment through visual, auditory and kinesthetic senses and the output is the decisions we take after the input is processed through our belief system.

Input	Visual, Auditory & Kinesthetic sources
↓	↓
Computer	Human body
↓	↓
Software	Belief System
↓	↓
Output	Decisions and Performance

Figure: Process of how we take decisions on a daily basis.
Our belief system being the software which processes our inputs

Challenge for us is to change the existing virus ridden softwares and install new softwares every time. On a long term basis surpassing our beliefs gradually take us to a new rich life, which is analogous to upgrading your newly installed software daily. Imagine how would you feel, how much energy will be at your hands, the abundance of resources you will tap once your mind starts processing with your newly found belief software thereby changing your outcomes so fast. The quality of your beliefs will determine the quality of your actions.

To get extra-ordinary results there is a need to see, hear and feel yourself breaking your belief barriers – experience it in your mind. Change your input to change your output.

The Secret Lies in Affirmations

The only communication which happens twenty four hours a day is internal communication. We are doing it both in our sleep and waking time with the most complex yet omnipotent creation of our body called the mind. Our mind is always in the driver's seat and is guiding us towards and away from several life situations – positive and negative. We would be happy to have it as our driver if it is good and credible, but if it is dangerous it would consistently put us into trouble every time and we would always be wary of its capability to help us reach home. We as individuals have the authority to train our mind at our will. As we know that one thing which happens almost twenty four hours is our continuous communication with our mind, we have the license to mold the mind and correct it whenever we see that it is not working for us. The process is called Affirmations! Affirmations can evolve a mind and bring it back to the tracks you laid for your Success. Go get your car running !

You do it all the Time

"You are today where your thoughts have brought you; you will be tomorrow where your thoughts take you."

James Allen

Remember the time when you were a kid running a race with your friends. You saw that your friends were doing very well, they had covered half the ground but you had hardly covered one fourth of it. What did you do? You would have reacted to it in two ways either you would have given up or you would have had a dialogue with yourself saying "I can do it, I can do it, I will run faster, I will increase my speed, I will reach...." You repeatedly made positive statements to yourself to make your mind into a driving force for your body. And you would have surprisingly seen that with this self talk, there was an improvement in your performance because this internal dialogue was a command you gave to your mind.

If we observe our behavior while we are engaged in something which we don't find interesting we will notice that we consistently send commands to our mind to stay focused on the task. For example we have an internal dialogue with ourselves which sounds like this – "Keep your attention for some more time, it's just a matter of ten minutes, I can do it...." This shows that our internal dialogue with our minds helps us perform more than we could in reality. The question is when we know there is so much of untapped energy, potential, stamina in our body, how to utilize it to the fullest with least resistance. The answer lies in Affirmations.

Affirmations are positive statements of a desired situation, repeated consistently to the mind aimed at enhancing our ability to reach a productive state of achievement. Affirmations work on both – our conscious and subconscious mind to make the desired changes we require in becoming successful.

Positive self talk has a direct connection with your performance – it is like having a catalogue, you ask for it and it is given.

Our mental Odyssey:
Conscious to Sub-Conscious

"Once you learn to do something consciously, you can move it into the subconscious and do it well. Everything you do well will be done subconsciously."

Zig Ziglar

All our behaviors, actions, thoughts and feelings are first experienced by our conscious mind and then our sub-conscious mind. This is the way we learn to do things. Recall the time when you first started to learn to drive. When you sat in the driving seat the first time, you were aware of your surroundings and you wanted to focus on the task at hand i.e. driving. You were *conscious* of how much pressure to be applied to the accelerator, on the change of gears, carefully following the instructions of your mind. Suddenly you saw a dog passing by in front and you *consciously* made the adequate changes – you lowered your gear, sending a message to your feet to get off the race pedal and move to the brake while applying gradual pressure on it. You were *conscious* of almost every moment you made while sitting in the driving seat. After few more repeated practice sessions, your desired actions and behaviors percolated to your sub-conscious mind and then there was no need for you to take any action consciously, because the desired behavior became a part of the sub-conscious which operates in background. Similarly when you begin to consciously impress the sub-conscious mind with positive statements repeated regularly for the desired result, it will gradually make a mark on your sub-conscious making it possible for you to gain the productive state at sub-conscious level with least resistance.

When you say to yourself consciously "you can do it" repeatedly it will make a dent in your sub-conscious and will become an unquestionable command to your mind to illicit the desired behavior, action, thought and feeling whatever that helps you perform at an extra-ordinary level.

MOHAMMAD ALI-The Legend

Not many know the story behind the man who was born in Kentucky in 1942. He was the three time heavy weight boxing champion and regarded as the Greatest boxer of all times. He believed in a powerful tool which amazed people to an extent that it became a popular tool in achieving extra ordinary results in any sphere of life. This was called the power of Affirmations. Even before he won the World Champion, he used to say "I am the Greatest, I am the Champion" – this statement acted as a command for his subconscious making him believe he was the greatest, and then his nervous system responded to his command by making appropriate changes in his body – the way he felt, the way he talked and the way he fought. That is what made the difference. He was so adept at using Affirmations that he went a step ahead and began to affirm the round in which he will beat his opponent. And to the surprise of audiences, he did exactly that. He beat his opponents in the round he affirmed. That is the power of Affirmations.

Affirmation as a tool is neutral to everyone. Its effects can be both positive and negative, depending on the type of affirmation process you are having with yourself. You focus on having a positive conversation with your mind, you will get positive results through your actions and if you have a negative communication process going on, your results will be negative. It gives equal opportunity to make your life as beautiful as you want and as hell as you like it to be. You might have seen people who are always complaining about their circumstances, they do it repeatedly and impress their sub-conscious mind with all kinds of complaints. Once this pattern of complaints sets in the sub-conscious, it will begin acting at a level where you will be complaining of almost everything that comes across or happens to you. Without consciously thinking about the scenario your sub-conscious will come up with questions that will direct you to think to complain on every aspect thereby losing out what is best for you in that situation. This can be counterproductive if you are looking at getting positive results in your life.

Whatever you affirm consciously and with a consistent repetition will be picked up by the sub-conscious – which will then manifest it in your life.

Let your mind Record your Own Voice

"The ancestor of every action is a thought."
Ralph Waldo Emerson

Let us imagine if we switch on the voice recorder at a busy bus terminal; it will record all kinds of voices which occur in the vicinity. It will not make any judgments as to which voice is good or which is bad, which is to be recorded and which is to be left. The voices may be of few people fighting amongst themselves, people discussing what is possible and what is not in our world, people undermining each other's potential, validating weaknesses of each other, demeaning some other person who has nothing to do with them and many others noises and disturbances which strike the mike's recorder. All these will be recorded in the tape. Your sub-conscious mind is similar to that recorder and it records all kinds of beliefs, thoughts, actions and feelings which occur in your surroundings without letting you know that it is been recorded. And as a result this recording will be manifested in your actions and the way you feel on a daily basis and affect the quality of results you get.

The way your heart pumps, the way brain sends signals to various body parts, examples such as these are nothing but sub-conscious actions of your body. You don't tell your body to breath or your heart to pump blood across the body, you never remain conscious when you brush your teeth or tie your shoe lace nor you are conscious in driving your car or riding a bike-control is with the sub-conscious. You do all these activities

with the help of your sub-conscious mind.

Recall the time when you were deeply engrossed in your reading and suddenly your hands move out to your neck for itching and you continue consciously reading the material. Recall the time when you were driving your car and also talking with your friend sitting beside you, with one hand you are also changing the radio station, and also having a look at a beautiful girl passing by across the road. How can you do so many activities while you are driving your car? It is because you are driving sub-consciously, you never tell your feet to apply this much amount of pressure or now is the time to change the gear or move the steering – it's all the part of your sub-conscious mind. The conscious mind averages only 2,000 bits of information per second while the sub-conscious mind processes at 4 billion bits per second on average! That is the power your sub- conscious wields.

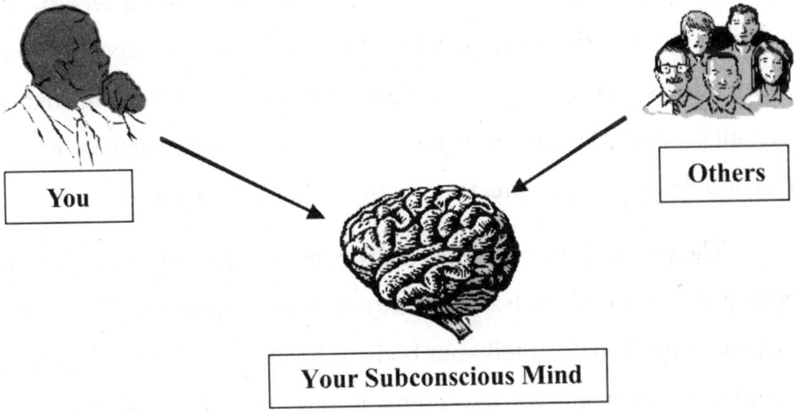

Figure: How you and others are shaping your sub-conscious mind on a daily basis

Affirmations occur every moment – they can either be triggered by you or others. The choice lies with you how you would like to shape and utilize this part of the mind which has tremendous untapped potential.

Affirmations are also called suggestions. If you suggest anything to your mind the process is called auto suggestion and if others program your mind it is called hetero suggestion. There is no harm in both of them, till they are done to get maximum positive results. Hetero suggestion is very common and we do it almost every time. Recall the time when your mom used to ask you to study, your teacher telling you to concentrate while you are in the class, reading a romantic magazine, watching television news et al – all these are examples of hetero suggestion.

Be selective in hetero suggestion and never let any negativity impress your sub conscious mind or it will affect the way you get results in your life. The way to change the quality of hetero suggestion is to change the inputs to your mind. Making sure that only empowering suggestion goes to your mind is an easy way to take advantage of this channel. You can get amazing results through hetero suggestion when you follow the following principles:

1. Communicate with possibility – people (PP). They are those people who always look out for possibilities in life instead of impossibilities which do not exists. They encourage themselves and others to go beyond the obvious and find their potential. With some people you feel empowered because they will let you be who you are, they will show belief in your capacities and strengths, always boosting your potential and pushing limits for you. Be with them.

2.Read Self-Development books – Read as much as you can, but read selectively. Any book which gives you an idea to succeed or gives you motivation to live fully will help you transform your life. Reading autobiographies is another way to communicate with the leaders of the World. It is just like having a conversation with them – you exchanging your thoughts with them and they will be sharing their thoughts with you – just like an idea exchange program. It's a process of having positive affirmations through the right resources. There is so much for you to experience but there is no need to experience everything – rather we need to learn from others mistakes because we will not live to gain all the experiences of the world. There are techniques, methods, and processes of all kinds that explain how to get rid of any fear you have. If you wish to achieve anything in your life find the book which assists you in developing the right potential that will help you reach your destiny and hence have a positive effect on your mind.

3.Listen to audio tapes: Why waste time when traveling. Seeing and hearing all the crap which is happening around you thereby letting these hetero suggestions take a toll on your inner belief system. It was found in the study that on an average a person travels almost three to four hours a day, which is approximately 1277 hours in a year equivalent to 53 days or close to two months. We know the difference between an Olympic winner and the one next to him is miniscule and in life too the difference between extra ordinary success and success is also very less. When people are having twelve months at their hands you will be having fourteen months, only if you recognize the value of the two extra months that you get. Use this time to listen to audio tapes on subjects like motivation, leadership, success, performance, belief, love, passion and many more. Nowadays one has so many audio programs available to develop your skills and talents-search "audio tapes" on Google and you will get about 7,050,000 results. Download podcasts of people you like to hear. Something that I would recommend listening to are podcasts of Robin Sharma, Jack Canfield and many other leadership gurus, their insights on the subject are amazingly helpful. Keep audio cassettes, CDs, pen drives on the move that will freshen up your thinking on the go.

Autosuggestion is much more powerful than Hetero suggestion because it is driven by your own mind and not of others. So you have a choice of thought and level of intensity with which you may suggest to your subconscious mind. And the funny part is that auto suggestion happens almost all the time except the time you are asleep. When you talk, your subconscious listens, when you shout in anger your subconscious listens, when you praise someone your subconscious listens. It is active all the time. Our self talk significantly affects the behavior we possess – affirmation is a process to turn your inner ghost into an inner angel which will not only guard you from negative thoughts but also energize you with abundance of positivity and hence change your behavior. Hence it is important for us to watch what we say to ourselves and others around us, as it affects your conditioning. And the most interesting thing is that if you don't suggest to yourself then people will start suggesting to you i.e. if you don't condition your mind the way you want then others will do it according to what they want.

One of the leading Self-help Gurus, Tony Robbins, says, "All personal changes must take place at the sub-conscious level." Challenge for us is to get rid of the already written and wired thoughts and create a new wiring of positive and more empowering thoughts. In a computer, you write something and then press the delete button to delete it, but in our mind you write something and only way to delete is to write something over it – i.e. Overwrite.

Autosuggestion and Hetero suggestion are the radical success tools to make the changes you desired in your life.

The Recipe to craft Winning Affirmations

"You will be a failure, until you impress the subconscious with the conviction that you are a success. This is done by making an affirmation which clicks."

Florence Scovel Shinn

1. Must be stated in the Positive sense: The affirmative statements must not have negations in them. Let us take an example of an affirmation "I will not be angry". This affirmation's purpose is to make sure that anger does not get on to the mind. Here the person says to himself repeatedly a statement with the aim that it will reduce his anger. But somehow he doesn't understand the biological flaw of our subconscious mind – that it does not understand negations. For example read this statement and think about it – "Don't think about the yellow elephant". Now when you say this statement to your mind, you thought about the yellow elephant. This is how our mind works – It will first think about the yellow elephant and then put a blank screen in your mind that you do not have to think about it, which means that you actually thought about what you negated. So many people use affirmations which are incorrect, for example – I will not smoke, I don't like to drink, I won't stress myself, I will never complain, I will stop teasing my friends. But now you know what kind of message you are sending to your brain when you make such statements to yourself – they will have an opposite effect. It is because of the simple reason that our subconscious doesn't understand negations.

2. Affirmation should be in the Present tense: Most of times, we live in the past which keeps on driving us forward. This is like putting the

reverse gear of your car and trying to move ahead, it is like moving forward by looking at the rear view mirror. We say to ourselves – I was like this since I was born, I was that since that time. It is just like saying to yourself, "I will remain as I was in the past". But the irony is that if you remain as you were you will become as you are. To change the outcomes of your life, you need to change your present first.

Affirmation focused on the future is as dis-empowering as an affirmation of the past. Let us make a simple affirmation for confidence – "I will become highly confident". If you analyze the statement, it says you will become confident, which looks like a future prediction for us. Now remember the time when you were a child you used to say, "I will become a doctor, I will become a civil servant, I will become a fighter pilot and so on." All of these are mere future predictions, which lacked conviction and commitment in them – they lacked power. If you say you want to become something, you create a big gap between where you are now and where you want to be and this gap remains as such, irrespective of the time which is passing on. Today you say you want to become confident and after a year too you are saying the same statement, so where is the change you want to see? You wanted to become confident and if after a year you still aim to become confident, there is no difference. To change your output in life, you must change the inputs to your mind right away in the present. Affirmations should be placed in present tenses which are in line with the outcomes you wish to have in your life. For example you wish to affirm your mind of confidence, an affirmation could be – I feel confidence in every cell of my body or I feel the burst of confidence in me or I am the confidence I desire or I accomplish anything I put my mind on.

Affirmations which contain the word "want" are also not powerful because they create want and not the feeling you desire. You say, "I want to become confident" or "I want financial abundance" – first of all it is stated in future tense and when you say you want something the subconscious mind craves for more want and in the process it is stuck in a situation of desire and want. Instead you should like your body and mind to experience the emotion you desire right now rather than waiting for the right time.

The affirmations should be stated in positive present tense, which gives your mind a direct command of the feeling you desire. It is a process of creating urgency for your subconscious mind right now, in this present moment. Structuring the affirmation that the result is already here is more powerful than any other affirmation.

Any thought in the Positive Present state yields more power than any other thought which strikes your mind – allow only positive present ideas to your mind.

How to use Affirmation

"It's the repetition of affirmations that leads to belief. And once that belief becomes a deep conviction, things begin to happen."

Claude M. Bristol

1. Believe: Any inconsistency in the affirmation with your belief will cause a delay in manifestation of the desired experience. Initially when you begin the process of affirmation there is going to be a misalignment of your mind and your subconscious, but the misalignment is temporary. It is like mining gold – the more you chip away the rocks the more gold you are going to find, the only thing is that you need to mine at the right place. Your mind is already a gold mine waiting to be mined; it wants you to chip away the resistance in the form of negative beliefs implanted by our seemingly negative world. Keep on chipping away the resistance with repeated blows of strong empowering fresh omnipotent affirmations. If you play tennis, you will know how the process takes place. Initially when you are an amateur, there will be a great deal of difficulty while hitting the ball because you are not comfortable with the idea of hitting a ball with a racket. But with conscious practice and awareness you develop the skill of hitting the ball without even seeing the ball. Same goes with affirmations – you will experience resistance during the beginning but as you go on enjoying the process, you will liberate yourself from your dis-empowering attitudes and enjoy the benefits of affirmations. Believe in the affirmation that it is manifesting in your life and plays a major role in attracting in your life

what you desire. Affirmation is the first step towards receiving what you always wanted in life.

2. Repeat: Repetition is the key to the whole process. It is like making a dent in your negative belief system which has created boundaries to your potential, a process of making way to your unlimited capacities that you possess and a path of rejuvenation that aligns your skills and talents with your dreams. The way we develop muscles in our body is similar to the way we develop a desired experience in our mind. When you go the gym for the first time, you don't expect to develop your muscles immediately. When you reach home after the first day at the gym and wake up the next morning you have complete body ache, and it is because this is the first time you have exercised your muscles. Similarly when you exercise your mind with repeated affirmations you will feel a contradiction. Recognize that contradiction is the first step to develop your potential. You go to the gym regularly thereafter and begin to see the changes in your body structure, your body responds to the repeated exercises which revitalize the unused muscles. Your affirmations create motion in your mind and create the activity which makes your belief system stronger and stronger, empowering every neuron of your brain, until the time when you see yourself totally in shape. Let us take the example of a swimmer. Do you believe he became an expert in his first swim – the answer is no. Initially he would have found it extremely arduous to keep himself afloat, and not only that, he might have faced a difficulty in breathing too. It is only when he repeatedly practiced his diving and swimming skills that swimming became an inherent part of his mental model and he thereby became

competent in the sport. It is the repetition that brings about results. And on the same lines it is the Repetition that is the key to successful affirmations.

3. Use: When you need the experience you desire which you have been affirming, affirm just before the time you require yourself to perform. It is nothing but a booster you give yourself. Remember how Americans accomplished their dream of going to the moon with the Apollo 11 mission on July 20, 1969 when astronauts Neil Armstrong and Buzz Aldrin landed on the Moon. Apollo 11 had to burn its boosters to travel through the gravitational field of the Earth just after it took off. Without the boosters firing at the right time, it would have been difficult for the Americans to accomplish their dream. To fire your boosters of performance, use affirmations whenever possible if you are committed to crossing the negative belief field and reach the place where you had dreamt of.

4. Act: Someone said "Logic will not change an emotion only motion can change emotion". Action preceded by affirmation is a deadly weapon which can fire your potential to a great extent. Action according to the belief brings in results you desire in your life. If you affirm yourself to love, your affirmation maybe – I right now express the love to all those I meet. You instilled a belief that you love, and then you repeated it as many times, after which comes the time to use it when you desire the feeling/experience. The last step you need to follow is to act according to the belief you had affirmed yourself. Act as if you feel love in every cell of your being, as if you are radiating a feeling of love with every person

you meet. Act your affirmation in the real world and it will change the way you feel inside remember your mind controls your body but the reverse is also true. It is the application of affirmation (AOA) that will begin the process of changes to get aligned with your ultimate desire.

Formula: BELIEVE →REPEAT→USE →ACT

Powerful Affirmations for every sphere of Life

Love

1. The more I love people, the more I love MYSELF
2. My loving relationships are long lasting, replete with LOVE
3. EVERY DAY in every way I am receiving love from people
4. I am a loving angel who spreads unconditional love EFFORTLESSLY
5. I am ALREADY receiving joy, love and compassion everyday every second

Forgiveness

1. The door to MYSELF opens when I forgive
2. I forgive, I forgive and I forgive and as I forgive, I HEAL
3. I RELEASE my past to begin my love filled future
4. Forgiving makes me FREE as a bird
5. I forgive the past, the present and future and LIBERATE myself

Courage

1. I face failure or success with my COURAGE
2. My courage allows me to become FEARLESS and DARING
3. I overcome my fears with my INNER courage
4. Every breath I take is replete with a courageous FORCE
5. Like a lion, I CHOOSE to be courageous

Success

1. I create ABUNDANCE in my life through my work
2. I allow myself to contribute tremendous VALUE to what I do
3. I ATTRACT success in whatever I do
4. I forge lasting WINS with my consistent effort
5. I use my ENDLESS capacities to get sustainable success

Wealth

1. The more value I add to people, the more financially ABUNDANT I become
2. I accomplish my GOALS to attract abundance
3. I have THE RIGHT to become amazingly rich
4. I visualize abundance for myself and OTHERS
5. I attract money and people with the WORK I do

Focusing and Attracting Your Desired Life

Our brain has been the most mysterious subject studied in medical sciences. We have always known the famous ten percent rule since we were a child and our Grandma used to tell us when we sat to study that it was only Einstein and a few other great scientists, philosophers and leaders of their field, who were able to use ten percent of their brain, and rest of us used much less than that. It would be a breakthrough in human performance if we get to know the way our brain works and how to extract the benefit of its biological working to maximize our performance.

We attract what we Focus on

"Formulate and stamp indelibly on your mind a mental picture of yourself as succeeding. Hold this picture tenaciously. Never permit it to fade. Your mind will seek to develop the picture."

Norman Vincent Peale

Our mind will attract only those things in our lives which we have put focus on. If you focus on happiness you will get happiness, if you focus on pain you will receive pain. It is a simple formula of "like attracting like". Let us take an example which you can yourself try out – when you are driving a car or motorbike on a straight road, with your eyes on the road, shift your focus from the center to either right or left. You will be surprised to see that your vehicle starts to move automatically in the direction you focus on, as your hands will begin to turn the steering wheel towards that direction on a subconscious level, without you knowing it. This process started consciously when you began to focus and within no time, your subconscious made all the physiological changes required to get aligned to your focus. It proves that if our mind is focused on anything, our actions and energy starts flowing towards it without you knowing about it.

Imagine yourself having a goal in your life which you wish to accomplish but somehow you are not able to focus your energies towards its fulfillment. Just start focusing on the goal with all your attention regularly. Think about that goal, talk about it with people and focus on how you will feel on accomplishing the goal. Your mind will start making the changes required in every aspect of your life from your behavior to your actions to your thoughts, which will make you reach the goal in the fastest and most harmonious way possible.

Let us take a simple and most common example of getting it right in achieving a goal through focus – suppose you wish to buy a car. Let us assume you wish for a Mercedes E-class Coupe. First you thought that that is the car you need to have with you. Before the purchase and after the time you focused your mind on purchasing a Mercedes E-class Coupe, when you move across the roads you will see this car everywhere, you move across any parking area, what you see is a Mercedes E-class Coupe, you are going for a jog and again you see a Mercedes E-class Coupe moving around. How is it possible that at so many places and among so many cars you are able to spot a Mercedes E-class Coupe everywhere you go? It is because our mind has the power to align the physiology to what the mind focuses on.

Your physiology is in direct control of your subconscious – focus your subconscious to a target and your physiology begins to change.

Our Mind has all the Answers

"What we think determines what happens to us, so if we want to change our lives, we need to stretch our minds."

Wayne Dyer

Let me ask you a question – If you were asked to advice a man, who is presently having no money, to travel from New Delhi to London, are there any possibilities? Ask this question to your mind and it will give you a Yes. It will give you various solutions – he can work and earn money, travel through a boat while serving as a workman, he may borrow money, or he may reach there through illegal means. The point I am trying to make is that irrespective of the resources available, your mind has an ability to find ways for you to reach your destination. What is really important for the mind to work this way and give you solutions, is that you need to feed it with a destination, a target which you wish to achieve. Feeding your mind with a goal is the most important step for gaining insights, solutions and processes to reach your goal.

Our mind is so innovative and creative that it already has all the solutions to problems that exist in this world, the only task is to act out the solutions in the real world, get results and again ask your mind for further direction. I will share an exercise which I use in my programs. I ask participants a question. Question is "How will a man cross a river which is 20 feet wide when he has nothing at hand?" The participants will come with all sorts of solutions like he will make a boat with the wood available, swim the river to the other end, take the support of a tyre or a floating object and flow through, cut a big tree which will act as a bridge to the other side and many others. This proves that our mind is innovative and creative once you give it a goal. Next I ask them another question and that is where the magic lies, asking them "How can he not reach the destination?" and again this time too participants gave all sorts of answers – the man will go blind, the river overflows, he injures himself while making the boat, the boat breaks in the river and many other impossibilities. This proves a wonderful point that irrespective of the resources available, your brain can align itself to the destination you wish to reach and give you customized solutions to your problem. I will ask you to do a similar but different exercise – answer this question, "Prove that you are Intelligent". You have to prove it irrespective of the reality of the statement – though it's very funny. Ask this question to your mind and it will give you all the logic you need to prove that you are intelligent. And again now ask another question to your mind "Prove that you are not intelligent", and you will be surprised that your mind answers that question equally well. It will again give you all the insights you need to prove that you are not intelligent. It is because our mind has all the answers you are looking for in your life, the only thing matters is where we put our focus on.

If you wish to test your mind's solution finding ability, you can do it right now – Close your eyes and ask it any question for which you are looking for a solution. And there will be a voice that will come from inside which will provide you with all kinds of solutions. The problem with us is that we never ask our mind for solutions, but ask it to rerun our negative experiences again and again making us feel dis-empowered. We get stuck in the problem and our mind's focus becomes the problem and not the solution and hence we stay at the same place. It is anytime better to ask for solutions and implement them as quickly as possible to overcome the challenges you are facing. Our brain is nothing but a radar in the sea of challenges which will guide the ship of your body to reach the destination you decide to conquer. It will tell you where is north, west, south, east and let you know the fastest way to your target.

Your mind has answers to all the questions you will ever have about Your life – it is an inner voice which guides you at every moment. Recognize it and let it show the light to you.

Getting results through Controlled Focus

"What matters is where you want to go. Focus in the right direction!"

Donald Trump

We have read the old traditional example of focus which states that when the magnifying glass is placed under the sunlight, it gains the capacity to burn what is beneath it through the power of controlled focus. This principle is still true and would be taken as a precedent for a long time. Controlled focus has the capacity to affect changes you require to make in the quality of your Performance.

You have been provided with five forces which carry tremendous potential to make long lasting changes in your life making you live your life on your own terms. The five forces which are always at your disposal are Emotional, Intellectual, Spiritual, Physiological and Physical energies.

P– Physical
E– Emotional
P– Physiological
S– Spiritual
I– Intellectual

A pneumonic for our resources is PEPSI – Physical, Emotional, Physiological, Spiritual and Intellectual. Your PEPSI energies will empower you in making you move from where you are to where you want to be, with tremendous drive.

Let us say that you have a goal to become the Vice President of a company you have just joined. Your aim is to reach your goal in five years. Use your Intellectual capacity to ask how to reach the goal with the resources you have now. Your mind will give you all kinds of actions and strategies which assist you in reaching your goal. It will provide you with the actions you need to take on a daily, weekly, monthly and yearly basis to fasten your progress; it will give you the resources you will need and the way to acquire them in the quickest possible manner; it will give you a list of people who could help you in your progress etc. It will give you your sub-goals, which will act as your stepping stones to success. But alone logic will not do much. We are excellent planners but planning does not get the results alone. Taking action is the next step you take to implement the solutions provided to you by your Intellectual resource. Action is not merely action in mind but Physical action and hence there is need to move. Move from where you are to where you see yourself, the journey is long and it is worth the learning. If you are thirsty and have a desire to quench your thirst, you will not only need the plan to get to the drinking resource but will also have to move your body into action in accordance with the plan, to reach the place and quench your thirst. We are successfully harnessing the two resources available right now to us – Intellectual and Physical. Sustaining your development would need a drive which if internal can give you the booster to sustain your capacities for long and make you persist in your drive – here comes the role of our Emotional resource. Need for knowing why you want the goal gives you insights on your emotions. Let us take for example a person who wants to earn big money, he actually doesn't want money but he desires a feeling of abundance, a person who has an aim to become a CEO, is driven by a desire to influence, a person who wants to write a book is driven by a desire to help people. Every goal of yours in materialistic terms or in physical world has its origin in a feeling which you long for. You don't need materialistic objects to satisfy yourself, it's a feeling which you long for. These physical objects are just a means for you to reach you to the feeling. Knowing the feeling that motivates you, will give you the drive you need to sustain your physical and intellectual efforts on a long term basis. When you have known the emotion which drives you, maximize that emotion whenever possible. Use tools such as visualization, as if principle, affirmations to enhance the emotion in your body. Once you have done that it will be like a positive force which will guide you through the process of achievement. Till now we have known four things:

1. Our Ultimate Outcome
2. A plan to reach the goal: Intellectual Capacity
3. Taking action on the plan: Physical Capacity
4. The motivation that drives us – emotion: Emotional Leverage

In this journey, you will feel like giving up many a times, because it will seem very arduous to keep moving on. The more you move closer to your goal, more difficult the journey becomes. Intellectual, physical and emotional capacities take you on the right track. But do you think these are the only powers available to you. The answer is no, because we have yet to use an effective strategy to success – our physiology. We have always said that our mind controls and drives our body, but the reverse is also true, as discussed in the previous chapters. Your actions will drive the emotion inside your body. Let us say you need to concentrate –

change your body posture and you will see the affect. Have you not wondered why yoga is done only in particular body postures called asanas – because the body changes help secrete certain chemicals in our body to reach a desired state. Remember the example of the teacher who is always saying to his students – "Sit up Straight". You may not be in sync with the desired qualities you need to achieve your goal, but changing your physiology by changing your actions and aligning them with your plan will bring in the requisite behavioral and thought outcome for your success.

The greatest force of our lives is our spiritual energy, the force which drives every organism on this planet, which has never been used in science of success. Have you thought of answering such questions for yourself – What is the purpose of your being, why are you here, what are you doing, where are you heading to? It is a pity that an adult finds it difficult to answer such simple basic questions about his/her life. Getting busy in achieving our goals is like traveling in your Mercedes without thinking of refueling it. Sooner or later it will run out of gas and you will be depleted of all the resources that have been working so well for you initially. To revitalize those resources, refuel them to full capacity, make use of your spiritual energy. Read spiritual books, listen to audio tapes, CDs etc and find out answers why your life is the way it is, why only a few events in your life are occurring again and again forming a pattern, what do you need to learn from them. See the patterns of your life, introspect and take control of all aspects of your life by focusing on them. Imagine a dart with two circles, a smaller circle placed in a bigger circle, inner circle representing the circle of Influence and the outer representing the circle of external environment – your job as a spiritual being is to focus on the circle of your influence, the things you have direct control on i.e. your actions, behaviors and thoughts and leave the circle of external environment as it is, because it is beyond your control. We always do the opposite, focusing on things which we can't control, attracting unhappiness in our lives daily, moment by moment.

Life is all about connecting the dots because every event that is happening in your life has a purpose, it has a meaning which will help you reach your goal faster and which will evolve you as a more spiritual human being. Once you connect all the dots, you will be able to see the whole picture describing you how the universe helped you reach your Goal.

All these five forces are gifted by the Universe only to make you aware that you are much more than yourself. We have never thought that we possess the powers beyond what we know, but the science of achievement has made it possible for us to get to know the origins and basics of Performance in our lives.

Use your PEPSI – Physical, Emotional, Physiological, Spiritual and Intellectual sources to quench your thirst for having your Ultimate life.

Our Mind can think only one thing at a Time

"Drag your thoughts away from your troubles... by the ears, by the heels, or any other way you can manage it."

Mark Twain

The greatest weakness of human mind is that it can think of only one thought at a moment. If you want to test it out yourself – Close your eyes and think of one pleasant experience you had in your life. Stop and then recall the most unpleasant experience you ever had in your life. Now the challenge for you is to recall both events simultaneously in your mind. Try it. Under no circumstance will you be able to recall both the experiences at one time. Because once you think of the positive experience the other thought will have to wait till you have finished feeling the first experience. Once you have finished with the first one, the second chosen thought will occupy your mind. Hence making it nearly impossible to feel both the thoughts at one time, which prove the fact that our focus determines which thought we hold and which thought we leave.

We also learn from this exercise why we feel grief or happiness. Once we are feeling happy because of a thought that happiness remains until we choose some other thought. If you remain in the first thought you will remain in the feeling. But once you choose another thought the feeling of the first thought goes away and the new feeling takes over. That explains why at a moment's notice we change how we feel – from positive to negative and negative to positive. Hence once you know that a thought of worry occupies your mind, it becomes difficult to get rid of that thought and feeling – how can a positive thought come in your mind till a negative thought is occupying it. Because for you to change the experience you will have to plant a new thought inside your mind, rooting out the old unpleasant thought. Only when you shift your focus from the negative to positive will you be able to change the feeling associated. It is like a game which you play with your brain, every moment in your life. If it gives the hot seat to a negative thought, don't give in. Rather remove the negative thought immediately and place your positive thought on your hot seat of the mind. The most interesting thing about the game is that you choose your win every time because you are far more proficient in regulating your brain. You just make a choice to place a thought you want and the negative thought will give way to it, it just cannot stop the thought supported by you for long.

You always play a game with your mind, it will put a negative thought and your duty will be to plant a positive one – who wins the game is the one whom you let.

Do you use your Reticular Activating System

"What you are is what you have been, and what you will be is what you do now."

Buddha

Reticular Activating System is that power of mind which makes the difference between your success and failure. It is a manually controlled system, but we let it run on an automatic mode, without leveraging the power it provides us. Being a filter between our conscious and sub conscious it empowers us to lead either a happy or a sad life depending on whether we are using it or not. Every successful man on this planet has used his or her RAS to his advantage to accomplish his goals.

RAS regulates our sleep and waking patterns, arousal, breathing and beating of the heart. But its prime function is to control the conscious mind because it has the ability to consciously focus your attention on something. It is like a filter to your inputs which are coming from VAK – Visual, Auditory and Kinesthetic senses. Do you know we are bombarded with approximately two million bits of information from our external environment – visual, olfactory, auditory, kinesthetic and gustatory? How do we handle so much information is a big question that haunts us. According to scientific studies, we can handle only seven new bits of information. This fact comes as a surprise to us when we know we are bombarded with huge chunks of information at any instant. What is the system that controls this information and directs only specific information to let in – it is our Reticular Activating System.

Think about a time when you were sitting at a railway station waiting for your train – you see so many people coming and going, luggage been loaded and unloaded, children crying, people talking with each other; you also hear lots of noises and sounds – voice of a cry, a couple fighting at the top of their voice, a tea seller asking people to buy tea; then there are so many types of smells – smell of the coffee, smell of the sweat of someone sitting beside you etc. And suddenly in all this commotion and variety of inputs – you hear your Train's name been called in the background. You hear it with absolute precision even when you are in a state where such large chunks of information are trying to get your mind's attention. That happens because of your reticular activating system being active – your RAS has indexed your train name in your sub conscious mind and it will automatically filter it as soon as it receives the train's name through the large information chunks which your conscious mind is receiving.

Your RAS is like a gatekeeper to your mental house, which will allow only those events or experiences to enter your mind which you have indexed or bookmarked or registered in the dairy of your RAS. You have the ability to program your RAS with consistent use of affirmations and visualization. The secret to use your RAS is to know that the happiest people on this planet have registered all the positive experiences they wish to experience in their RAS register and now it's the job of RAS to filter out from all the negative, neutral and positive experiences of their lives, only the positive ones which they have registered earlier and make it visible on the surface of your memories. That is why they see all the positivity spread over in their lives which others could not see. If you are not happy it doesn't mean that there is no happiness in your life, but it means you have not registered the right kind of experiences in your RAS. Unless you register those positive experiences which you desire most in life through use of techniques like affirmation and visualization, your RAS will keep on running on automatic mode keeping you at the same stage as you are and making you miss out on all the positivity life brings.

Applying RAS to goal setting is an excellent way to empower yourself with the right tools for achievement. When you feed your RAS with the goal you desire, it accepts and takes note of your goal thereby registering it. It is like telling your RAS the place where you wish to go, so now it is not your job but your RAS job to assist you in the process. It will automatically give your conscious mind the methods, tools and opportunities which will help you achieve your goal. It will find for you, all the resources that you need to hit your target from the information it gets bombarded with, every moment. It will filter out useful information and bring to the notice of your conscious mind the benefits and advantages of that information and how it will help you in achieving your goal. It is a magical device which empowers individuals in a big way only if we let it.

Register your thoughts, experiences and feelings in your RAS register and it will give you back the same thoughts, experiences and feelings in your Life – hence register carefully.

SELECT BIBLIOGRAPHY

1. Awaken the Giant Within,
Anthony Robbins

2. The User's Manual For The Brain,
Bob G, Bodenhamer, and L. Michael Hall

3. The Big Book of NLP Techniques,
Shlomo Vaknin

Wisdom Village (Publications Division)

WVPD

Knowledge is information. Wisdom is transformation.

Some Other Books by WVPD (WISDOM VILLAGE PUBLICATIONS DIVISION)

Broom & Groom
MRP Rs 195/-
(Kiran Bedi, PavanChoudary)

Art of Getting People To say yes
MRP 200/-
Arvinder Brara

When your are Sinking become a Submarine
MRP Rs 195/-
Pavan Choudary

Pavan Choudary

Chanakya's Political Wisdom
MPR Rs 100/- (HB)

Confucius' Social Wisdom
MPR Rs 100/-(HB)

Kabir's Spiritual Wisdom
MPR Rs 100/-(HB)

Success Sutras for the 21st Century
Set of 3 Books(HardBound) in a Box
MRP Rs 290/-

Healing in your Hands
(Acupressure)MRP Rs 250/-
Dr. Anand Verma

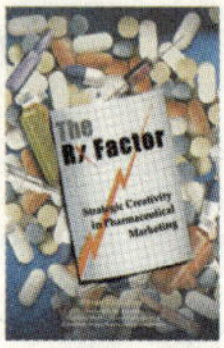

The Rx Factor
(Pharmaceutical Marketing-Reprint) MRP Rs 125/-
Pavan Choudary

Arise Awake
MRP Rs 225/-
Dr. P.V. Vaidyanathan

ORDER YOUR COPY. ON BULK ORDERS AVAIL SPECIAL DISCOUNT
CONTACT -+91 98108 00469, wvpdindia@gmail.com